THE OLD DAYS

WITH HORSE AND HOUND

being

THE STORY

of the

Chevy Chase Hunt

1892 - 1916

by

SAMUEL J. HENRY

No one ever came to grief except honourable grief through riding horses. No hour of life is lost that is spent in the saddle. Young men have often been ruined through owning horses, or through backing horses, but never through riding them; unless, of course, they break their necks, which taken at a gallop is a very good death to die.

—Sir Winston Churchill in *"My Early Life."*

FOREWORD

As an old fox hunter, now a little long in the tooth, I have derived a unique satisfaction in tracing the antecedents and history of the Chevy Chase Hunt with its famous horses and colorful personalities, its golden days, tragedies and inevitable passing; a sort of "running the heel" as it were, a term applied to hounds backtracking on the trail. Of course, no story of a hunting outfit, especially one that existed as far back as the Chevy Chase, would be authentic or even of much interest today without a fair evaluation of the sport, a bit of hunting verse and humor, as well as a few words on the background and environment beyond the doings of the Hunt itself. To cover this need I have endeavored, briefly, to bring to view appropriate vistas and persons that gave meaning and purpose to the Maryland countryside of a half century or more ago.

"It pleasures me," as the mountain folk say, to recall my first experience with the Hunt. On a crisp November day around the year 1901 I was cantering my horse, Dewey, on the Seventh Street Road (now Georgia Avenue) when the Hunt in all its dash and color hove in sight. It reminded me of scenes in Sir Walter Scott's novels of knights gathering for a tournament in the Medieval ages. When the prancing cavalcade reached the lands now occupied by the Walter Reed Hospital, the Huntsman turned off the road and led hounds and riders to a giant chestnut tree, which had been used by Union sharpshooters in the skirmishes around Fort Stevens in the Civil War. Then there were a couple of sharp notes from the horn and the Hunt was off, leaving me fascinated by the stirring pageant.

At that time I was a junior officer in the National Savings and Trust Company where Clarence Moore, Master of Fox Hounds of the Chevy Chase Hunt, kept his "Hunt Account," and I enjoyed chatting with Bob Curran, the Huntsman, when he came in to cash the weekly payroll check to pay the help at the kennels.

In addition to the Master and the Huntsman, I was also fortunate in the friendship of Woodbury and Gist Blair, George Howard and William B. Hibbs. Through these hospitable gentlemen, with whom I shared a deep interest in horses, I became acquainted with the sporting activities of the Club, although I did not become a member until some years later.

My thanks are extended to John M. Lynham, former President of the Club, for access to official records, and to Mrs. Arthur A. Snyder (one of the most skilled followers of the Chevy Chase Hounds) for refreshing my memory on many points and making available rare old data and photographs, as did Freddy Chapin, lately deceased, and Marrian L. Curran, son of the Huntsman.

Nor must I forget a word of appreciation to "Cap" Springirth, one time conductor on the Chevy Chase trolley line and later watchman in "The Village;" and to Mike Callaghan, nestor of local antiquarians born in a log cabin on Broad Branch Road in 1867, both of whom were mines of information on the history of the area. "A Sporting Family of the Old South" by my deceased friend Harry Worcester Smith, M.F.H., has been helpful in establishing a portion of the antecedents of the Hunt.

At this point there is a tribute due to a colorful group of members of the Chevy Chase Club who, calling themselves the Coursestormers, elected to publish this little book. I take it that their action was intended as a token of affection for the Queen of Clubs and I heartily salute their generous sentiments. The plan, which has now been executed, calls for the printing of 1,000 copies, 100 to be retained by the Coursestormers and the remaining

900 to be presented to the Club for distribution as the Board of Governors may decide.

Just one more thought before turning the hounds loose: This story, covering as it does merely one facet of the varied activities of the Chevy Chase Club, is intended only to supplement Mr. Lynham's comprehensive and richly illustrated volume "The Chevy Chase Club — A History," recently published.

January, 1960

Samuel J. Henry

Chevy Chase,

Maryland

Clarence Moore, M. F. H., Chevy Chase Hunt, 1899-1912.

The Old Days

"Tell me what men ye ar? he sayde,

Or whose men that ye be

Who gave youe leave to hunte in this

Chyviat Chays in the spyt of me?"

[Inscription over fireplace in the
taproom, Chevy Chase Club]

At the turn of the century, in what we affectionately call the old days, Washington was little more than a sleepy Southern town where whiskey sold for a dollar a quart, locusts droned their hot weather songs in the tree-lined streets, Saint Matthew's Church stood on the site of the Southern Building at Fifteenth and H Streets, N. W., and Theodore Roosevelt could frequently be seen galloping his horse in Rock Creek Park followed by a lone Cavalryman.

Out in Montgomery County, Maryland, Senator Newland's Chevy Chase Land Company was developing its large holdings and Mike Callaghan was making good money hauling gravel from Rock Creek. "Free enterprise" he called it. Now at 93, Mike, a great, rugged, deep-voiced man, enjoys recalling the old days. "Shure, I remember the Dumblane and the Chevy Chase Hunts," he says. "The Chevy Chase often galloped over my farm and the adjoining lands of the Cummings family, and to the north of us in the country beyond the Clean Drinking Manor on Jones Mill Road. Aye, and there was Clarence Moore always with a bill for a lad opening a gate, and the gentlemen in their silk hats and red coats, and the ladies, God bless 'em, with their little huntin' derbies and veils and riding habits, and Bob Curran racing along, a-whoopin' and a cappin' his hounds for'ard. Ah! it was wild, rare music to make your blood tingle."

Old Mike spoke truly, for in that remote and ancient period the Chevy Chase Club was the most popular rendezvous of the aristocratic fox hunting set of Washington and nearby Maryland and Virginia, and the old Bradley House saw many a gay party after the hunts when the riders and their friends gathered for the hunt breakfast, at which pink-whiskered Dr. Frank Loring, Chairman of the House Committee, acted as host and Gaskins, the jolly colored chef, served the refreshments. It was the custom to ride to hounds two or three times a week in season, when adventurous Dianas, sidesaddle, of course, and their hard-riding Squires, galloped cross-country to the exhilarating music of the full cry and challenge of the Huntsman's horn, the women asking no favors as they rode gayly up to the hounds to be in at the death, or if a drag hunt, to prove to the Master and his staff that they appreciated the efforts to show a good day's sport.

All in all, it was a lively, colorful era in the Club's history, when horse was king and hunting and racing were the main topics of conversation over tea cups or highballs, just as golf and tennis are nowadays; a creditable, if largely forgotten link in the long annals of sport in the Washington area, where riding to hounds appears to be as indigenous as honeysuckle vines or sassafras trees. To round out this rambling sketch, which aims to be a short history of the Hunt, a few words on its antecedents may be of interest to Club members, not forgetting a bow to the immortal fox hunter of Mount Vernon.

Old Stewart's Hot Punch

Around 1820, a quiet, genial old codger named Stewart, who lived on the scant earnings of two billiard tables, had a kennel of some seven or eight couples of native-bred hounds located on Fourteenth Street, south of the Avenue. Stewart, who hunted two or three times a week, was not a bold or hard rider, but so thorough was his knowledge of the country, his hounds and the game, he rarely missed being in at the death. Next to a good run, old Stewart's greatest delight was to be seated before a cheerful fire on a cold winter's evening with a jorum of screeching hot punch at his elbow, relating to his companions all of the minutest incidents of the chase and commenting on the individual conduct of each of his hounds.

The Washington Hunt

The regime of the Washington Hunt, in the 1830's, furnished the first organized fox hunting in the District of Columbia and nearby counties, Andrew Jackson giving dinners in the White House to celebrate noted chases. Regularly throughout the season, from November through March, a well-trained pack of hounds went out three times a week, meeting generally in Prince Georges and Fairfax counties in close vicinity of the city and sometimes in the District itself, where foxes — both red and gray — were found within hearing of the town bells.

Sir Charles Vaughan, the British Minister, a "fine English gentleman of the olden time," was president of the club, and Sir Andrew Buchanan and Mr. Pitt Adams, his secretaries of legation, were general managers and whippers-in. Under these gentlemen as kennel-keeper and first whip was Mason Clark, son-in-law of old Fuller who kept what later became Willard's Hotel. Not only all the young men, including the President's nephew Andrew Jackson Donelson, but even grave members of the Senate and House of Representatives and nearly all the Army, Navy and Marine Corps officers on duty in Washington were members.

Mason Clark and Whistle Jacket

Says an old chronicler, "It was a pleasant sight to witness, by the dim light of early day, a meeting of the club at the kennels, only a short distance across from Willard's and to follow the long procession across the bridge into Virginia. At the head was Mason Clark on his thoroughbred, a wiry little bay, 'Whistle Jacket,' followed in close order by 30 or 40 hounds in couples, and immediately in the rear the large 'field' of well-mounted gentlemen, doing the amiable to a lot of bright girls, most of them Southern-bred and, of course, capital horsewomen. Then the silent woods, covering the heights of Arlington, would become vocal when the cry of hounds announced the fox was away. The vociferous roar, on a still day, would be echoed under the White House portico, recalling to the President, no doubt, his younger days."

The Capitol in an Uproar

In one of its hunts the hounds got a fox on foot and ran into it near the Navy Yard, but the riders were wound up to such a high pitch they got to debating whether they should cross the Eastern Branch and try for a fox in Prince Georges County or cross the long bridge into Virginia, when the irrepressible Buchanan of the British Legation made fast one of his reins to the dead fox and galloped off, leaving orders with Clark to lay the hounds on after he had gone a mile. Buchanan made a beeline for Eckington, north of the city where the hunt had started, galloping across the Capitol plaza where the Supreme Court, Senate and House were all in session. When the mad freak of the irrepressible fox hunters brought the baying pack to the attention of the sedate judges and lawmakers, all the windows in front of the Capitol were thrown open and crowded with the amazed functionaries, and one enthusiastic fox hunter from the State of Mississippi rushed out bare-headed, leaped on a horse standing at the rack, and joined the outlandish race yelling like a wild Indian until the drag was run into at Eckington some four miles away.

Grocer Hoskins

In the 1870's, a grocer named Hoskins, who lived on Fourteenth Street, proved himself not only a businessman but also a sportsman. He kept his hounds in his back yard, delivered groceries by horse and wagon, and to the satisfaction of friends who loved to chase Brer Fox, saddled the same horse of afternoons to lead them in runs on adjoining farms. No pink coats — just well worn corduroy. (Reminds one of John Jorrocks, the fat, jolly grocer of London in the "Hunting Tours of Surtees," published about a hundred years ago in England.)

The Prince Georges

After old Hoskins, we come upon the faintest of trails in which the Prince Georges County Hunt Club of Washington emerges in the early 1880's, with its membership consisting of H. Rozier Dulany, Allan Arthur, Jesse Brown, Arthur Addison, Charles Thompson, George Hellen, E. C. Blunt and others. Dulany, Hellen, Addison and Brown, all of whom I came to know, would naturally be in it; they were sportsmen of the highest type, and nothing appealed to them more than a day with foxhounds, undoubtedly of the Maryland-Virginia breed.

The Dumblane Hunt

Samuel S. Howland, a well-known sportsman and brother-in-law of August Belmont, now comes on the scene. It was he who in 1885 organized the Dumblane Hunt and brought over what probably was the first pack of English hounds ever seen in this vicinity. For Master, George Eustis, a hearty, blue-eyed, red-faced man, who had hunted in Ireland and England, was named. The Huntsman, Charles Briscoe, came from a family of noted English huntsmen. Located in Tenleytown (or Tennallytown), D. C., in a building that still stands on the grounds of Immaculata Junior College, the Dumblane cut a wide swath in the social and sporting life of the period, many of the hunts ending at Grasslands, a pleasant retreat located near what is now Ward's Circle and adjoining the old Mount Vernon Seminary. At that time Grasslands was the home of William C. Whitney, Secretary of the Navy during President Grover Cleveland's first term (1885-1889), and the Secretary and his wife — who later met her death in a Virginia hunt — were subscribers to the Dumblane.

With Mr. Eustis as M.F.H., Briscoe hunted the Dumblane pack with considerable success, but after four years they gave up and in the winter of 1889 Mr. Howland, Mr. Dulany, Arthur Herbert, of the British Legation, and other gentlemen imported a second pack of English hounds. In this rejuvenation of Dumblane, Mr. Herbert was the first Master, next was Mr. Howland, and then Bob Neville an Irishman by birth but a Virginian by adoption.

9

This third and last M.F.H. of Dumblane was a strapping fellow and one of the handsomest men of his day; under him the hunt was quite popular. His Huntsman, brought from Ireland, was Alexander Walsh, likewise a big man standing six feet four inches. Acting as kennelman and whip was Bob Curran, a Tenleytown lad in his late 'teens. After two years Bob Neville, who had moved from Upperville, Virginia to Chevy Chase with his wife, the former Mary Dulany, found it necessary to resign as Master and his loss was keenly felt. The survivors of the old packs were sent to Grasslands where Mr. Howland then lived. As he was too busy to hunt much himself, a visiting Count de Jamtelle from Paris was named Honorary Huntsman and hunted the Dumblane through Prince Georges and Montgomery Counties. However, the Dumblane, having served its time, began to slacken its pace as if to make way for a youngster then being incubated.

Chevy Chase Club Organized

Plans for the Chevy Chase Club, which was organized in 1892 as a country club "with a hunting element," originated in the office of Harvey L. Page, an architect, with a number of gentlemen in attendance including Senator Newlands, Henry M. Earle and Mr. Dulany. Senator Newlands, who laid out Chevy Chase and was a prime mover in all its early activities, had married "the Rose of Sharon," daughter of the wealthy "King of Comstock" and owner of the famous Yellow Jack Mine in Nevada. The Senator had invested heavily in Chevy Chase property, his tract running from the District line far out to Chevy Chase Lake. The Club's first home was a house on the Goldsborough farm, half a mile west of the Chevy Chase Circle, which Senator Newlands' Chevy Chase Land Company had purchased as part of its holdings. Mr. Earle was the first Master of Hounds and George Ryder the first Huntsman, who at that time was teaching Senator Newlands' daughters how to ride. The Newlands family were very fond of Ryder, taking him with them on trips abroad and to their ranch in Nevada. He is said to have introduced polo in California. In his later years he taught scores of the children of the Diplomatic Corps and others how to ride and drive horses. His religious persuasion was Seventh Day Adventist; under no circumstances would he permit a horse in his stable to be saddled after sundown Friday up to sundown Saturday.

First Fatality

Our earliest episode concerns a hunting man who came to the fledgling club on a bitter cold day, booted and spurred for the chase. As the ground was frozen solid the hunt was called off. However, the eager gentleman ordered his horse and after a few turns in the paddock put his mount at a jump where the rider sustained a nasty fall. Shrugging off the apprehension of friends, he declared he felt all right and attended the luncheon that followed. In four days the poor fellow was dead from internal injuries.

Dumblane and Chevy Chase Merge

Since the Dumblane Hunt and the Chevy Chase Club were controlled by the same interests a merger was effected and shortly thereafter the Chevy Chase moved to the Bradley House as the tenant of Captain John F. Rodgers, U. S. Navy, Retired, taking the hounds with them. Eventually the Club purchased the property, Mr. Earle negotiating the deal and contributing his broker's commission to the Club. Our Mr. Earle was an all-around fellow, not only in the business and sporting world but in the social as well, leading

10

MEADOWBROOK HUNT
:N HEAD, LONG ISLAND, N.Y.

:EAM FIELD, GOLD STRIPE
AND LETTERING

BRANDYWINE HUNT
WESTCHESTER, PA.

CREAM FIELD, MAROON FOX
AND CROSSINGS, CREAM
LETTERING

GENESEE VALLEY HUNT
GENESEO, N.Y.

GREEN FIELD, GOLD STRIPE
AND BALLS, BLACK LETTERING

RADNOR HUNT
WHITE HORSE, PA.

REY FIELD, RED BORDER
)X HEAD AND LETTERING

MYOPIA HUNT
SOUTH HAMILTON, MASS

CREAM FIELD, RED FOX
HEAD, CROSSINGS AND
LETTERING

PINE HILL HUNT
FRONT ROYAL, VA.

RED AND BLACK
CHECKERED FIELD
AND LETTERING

GRAFTON HUNT
GRAFTON, MASS.

REEN FIELD, RED STRIPE
AND GOLD LETTERING

ROSE TREE HUNT . . . .
MEDIA, PA.

LAVENDER FIELD, GOLD
BORDER, GREY HOUND
HEAD AND LETTERING

MONMOUTH COUNTY HUNT
RED BANK, N.J.

RED FIELD, BLACK
CROSS AND GOLD
LETTERING

Shields of Chevy Chase's companion hunts. Drawn from the originals by Mrs. Henry Ravenel.

Robert M. Curran, Huntsman, 1899-1916. Courtesy Marrian D. Curran.

the cotillion in the great hunt ball shortly before Christmas, 1893. These hunt balls, as any man to hounds will tell you, are the best dances in the wide category of the light fantastic — provided, all and sundry have previously wined and dined in ample degree. The Huntsman and the two Whippers (all in pink) take station at the ballroom entrance and hand out copies of age-old hunting songs.

The popular ditty "We'll All Go Out Hunting Today" starts off this way:

> There is but one cure for all maladies sure,
> That reacheth the heart to its core,
> 'Tis the sound of the horn on a fine hunting morn,
> And where is the heart wishing more?

Another song is the old favorite "Drink Puppy Drink":

> Here's to the fox in his earth below the rocks!
> And here's to the line that we follow,
> Here's to the hound with his nose upon the ground,
> Though merrily we whoop, and we holla.
> Then drink, puppy, drink, and let every puppy drink,
> That is old enough to lap and to swallow,
> For he'll grow into a hound, so pass the bottle 'round,
> And merrily we'll whoop and we'll holla!

Around two o'clock in the morning the Huntsman sounds the "Gone Away" on his horn and the cotillion begins.

The Monmouth Visits Us

Meanwhile, P. F. Collier brought the Monmouth County, New Jersey, hounds, of which he was M.F.H., to Maryland, kennelled them at Chevy Chase and hunted them on alternate days with the Chevy Chase pack. Two such lively outfits as the Monmouth and Chevy Chase hunts coming together in the name of sport and good fellowship was cause for celebration; they danced long and joyously, they rode hard and sometimes recklessly, they craved daring action and they got it, subscribing unreservedly to the philosophy of Adam Lindsay Gordon, the English Sportsman-author:

> No game was ever worth a rap
> For a rational man to play
> In which no accident, no mishap,
> Could possibly find its way.

Well, with the hunt crowd now off and running, they decided to introduce stag hunting in the Washington area, no less. The Rider and Driver of January 6, 1894, tells the story:

"Two genuine Irish stags are now housed at the stables of the Chevy Chase Hunt Club, Washington, D. C., and in a short time will furnish sport for both hunters and onlookers. The stag is trained for his run by easy stages. After confinement for some days in a comfortable stable, with an attractive selection of food, he is taken a few hundred yards from the barn and turned loose. At the first fright he makes for his accustomed shelter, and the next day, when taken a little further off, he does the same thing. He is finally trained so that when taken five miles from the home stable and turned loose, at the first sound of the hounds he throws up his nose, takes a comprehensive sniff for his bearings, and starts straight across country for shelter. Given anything like a fair start, with a tolerably open country and no barbed wire fences, there is not a hound that can touch him in a five-mile dash. If the pack does pull him down, that is his fault, and it is that much more sport for the hunters; but the proceeding, as a whole, is about as humane a method of hunting as could be devised, some of the English hunt clubs having hunted one of their wary old stags as many as a hundred times, the work proving just enough to keep him in good healthy digestion and the sport for the hunters being unquestionable. With the stags have also arrived a pack of imported Irish hounds, eighteen couple in all, which will add greatly to the hunting strength of the pack already in the city. In connection with hunting in Washington, the Monmouth club has taken a clubhouse and stables in the neighborhood of the Chevy Chase Club. Some of the best hunters from the stud will be sent down to winter in Washington, where the mildness of the season has surprised all who have visited the city this winter.

A New Year's Meet

"The New Year's meet of the Chevy Chase and Monmouth Hunt was at Woodley Inn, Washington, D. C., at two o'clock. The road was filled with handsome rigs, and the verandas at the inn were crowded with spectators. A large number of riders were in pink, adding color to the scene, which was one of the liveliest in the riding line that has been seen about Washington. The day was not too cold for comfort, and though the ground was quite wet from the recent rain, it was only the better for the scent and not much the worse going. The hounds were cast in the field near the hotel and started on a drag trail of about four miles toward the clubhouse at Chevy Chase, where the fox was to be loosed after the horses had been warmed up. The pace was lively and some stiff fences met with. The pack crossed the Tennallytown road, most of the riders taking the fences in and out, and after a run of some distance in sight of the road, the course changed toward Rock Creek, where there was more than one rider that turned back and more that got the cold water above the girths. Mr. Earle, who was well up with the pack, attempted to ease his horse by jumping near the shore, and after going head and ears under, had a swimming match with his mount for the shore. Mr. Butterfield received a bad fall at one of the fences on the way to the clubhouse, and Mr. Stone was another of the unfortunates who, aside from getting a nasty fall at one of the jumps, lost his horse. The fox was loosed near the clubhouse as the field came up, and after giving the horses a breathing spell while Reynard got a fair start, they were away and after him again. He was killed in the field opposite the clubhouse in sight of the crowd on the terrace. The brush went to Miss George, of Baltimore, who was the first of the ladies in at the death. Among those who finished in the first field were Messrs. Butterfield, Wallach, William and Lewis Earle, Broome, Hooe, Stone, Brown, Merrill and Gosling, Miss Newlands, Miss George, the Misses Evans and Miss Davis. The second fox was loosed in the field north of the clubhouse and ran in a circle, leading the hunters a chase of about three miles and a half, and falling under the fangs of the pack almost at the spot where he had been loosed. The brush went to Miss Newlands, who was well up with the field. The last run of the day was followed by about half a dozen of the field, whose enthusiasm had not been damped by eight miles of hard work across the country. A drag was laid to the crest of a hill southwest of the clubhouse, and the fox was loosed with about fifteen minutes' start on the pack. He headed straight south, giving the riders a stiff in-and-out across the road west of Chevy Chase Circle, and then back again into the

Reno road, whence he was followed south almost to Tennallytown. But he had showed poor judgment in choosing his course, and by the time the foremost riders had caught up with him some of the vagrant dogs from the settlement had run him to earth, and the riders were barely in time to save the brush. The most of the field had turned back before the death to take part in the Gymkhana races at the club. Among those who followed the hunt from the road, and who afterwards witnessed the races, were Mr. Gebhard, Mr. and Mrs. Pell, of New York, the Misses Brice, Mr. and Mrs. Slack, Mr. and Mrs. Ffoulke, the Misses Patten, Mrs. Bougher, and Messrs. Washington, Phillip, Brice, McKenny, Redfern, Marrow, Barons Grip and von Kettler, Miss Kelton, Frank T. Rawlings, Miss Whiting, Mr. and Miss Darneille, Mr. and Miss Geyer, Robert Gibson, Miss Williams, Robert Reily, P. F. Collier, of New York and Clarence Moore."

The Rider and Driver comes up with more stories:

A Sporting Afternoon

"On Saturday last (January 13, 1894) the riders of the Chevy Chase Club and the members of the Monmouth County Hunt, whose stud has been quartered in Washington for some weeks past, joined forces in one of the liveliest cross-country runs of the season. A good field turned out for the meet, which was at Brightwood, Washington, D. C., at 3 p.m., and there was a much larger crowd at the Chevy Chase Club, where tea was served after the run and where Gymkhana races closed the day's sport. Out of the good field of starters, however, there was but a small proportion who followed straight over the course that had been laid by "Jimmy" Blute, the huntsman of the Monmouth pack. The Monmouth man tried himself in picking out one of the hardest routes that the Washington riders have followed this season, and he was strongly suspected of having laid a part of the trail from a boat, as it crossed Rock Creek three times in the course of the run.

"The day was a perfect one, warm and sunny as September, with the lately frozen ground just softened enough to hold the scent and making the going excellent. The cast was made at Takoma Park, four miles air line northeast of Chevy Chase. The trail headed direct for Rock Creek, where the take-off was a slide of six feet down the bank and a drop-off of three more into the icy water that took the horses above the girths. Fully a dozen of the field faced the music and swam their mounts across with the water above their boot tops. Miss Davis, who was the only lady in the field, gamely took the plunge with the rest and stayed with the huntsman straight to the finish.

"After crossing the creek the course turned west through part of Argyle, and then returning crossed the creek back and forth, the last take-off being over a barway into two feet of water, and landing the hunters on the west of the stream heading for the Chevy Chase Hotel. Here the pack caught the dragman, and there was a check of five minutes to breathe the horses. This was practically the end of the run, those finishing in the first flight being Miss Davis, Mr. Collins, Mr. Stone, Mr. Marrow and Mr. Evans. After the check there was a straightaway race for the Monmouth Kennels, a mile away, after which the party returned to the Chevy Chase clubhouse for tea.

"The gymkhana races included the egg and spoon race, the cigar and umbrella race, and a tandem race between Mr. Earle and Mr. Ryder, of the Chevy Chase Club, won by the former. The surprise of the occasion, however, was the winning of the half-mile flat for ponies 12 hands, one

15

inch and under by Master Sidney Holloway, aged twelve, who was riding his maiden race on a game little Indian pony, the smallest horse in the field.

"Among the guests of the afternoon and those who followed the run from the road were:

"Secretary Hoke Smith, Colonel and Mrs. Sweat, Woodbury Blair, Mr. Foulke, Fred McKenny, Mr. and Mrs. Carroll Mercer, Montgomery Blair, Mr. Butterfield, Mr. Manley, of Baltimore; Fred May, Mr. Steele, Robert Collins, Mr. Redfern, Mr. Broome, Mr. and Mrs. Clarence Moore, Admiral Jouett, Mr. and the Misses Newlands, the Misses Mendoca, James G. Blaine, Jr., Miss Kelton, Miss Deering, Miss Davis, Miss Conde Smith, Dr. Ritchie, the Misses Boardman, Miss Marrow, Horace Washington, Van Ness Philip, Miss Philip, Mrs. Hunt, and Mrs. Arnold."

In the issue of January 27, 1894, there is a story of a combined drag hunt with the Monmouth County hounds on Saturday, January 20, "finishing with a three-quarter mile dash after their stag, who took everything between the Chevy Chase clubhouse and his stable."

This article also refers to the Chevy Chase men taking up polo: "Some polo ponies are already there, and more are on the way. The grounds are being put in shape, and shortly there will be a match with the Baltimore men." All of which indicates that polo was actually introduced to Washington by Chevy Chase in the spring of 1894.

Mr. Collier Returns Home

Mr. Collier and the Monmouth Hunt remained with us for two years, when Mr. Earle moved to Long Island to join the fast-moving polo set and Mr. Collier and his hounds returned home. From 1896 to 1898 Colonel George M. Dunn led the field until he galloped off with Theodore Roosevelt and his Rough Riders to fight in the Spanish American War. Colonel Dunn was reputed to be the best dressed officer in the Army. Then once again Mr. Howland took over and with George Holloway as Huntsman the hunt showed renewed life. The next and greatest factor in the hunting activities was Clarence Moore who, in 1899, was elected Master.

Clarence Moore, before coming to Washington, was an unknown West Virginia stock broker. He took as his second wife the stunning black haired Maybelle Swift (of the packing family), acquired an interest in W. B. Hibbs & Co., and became obsessed with the idea of founding the finest stable of heavy weight hunters and the best pack of hounds in the country. The Huntsman he selected for the Chevy Chase pack, Bob Curran, who had served with the Dumblane and also with the Chevy Chase after the merger, was as brilliant in his line as the Master. Together they made the hunt stand out, although some sportsmen grumbled that the meets were too social and the hunts usually drags.

Scarlet and Black Selected

The Chevy Chase Hunt, moving into its finest era, now reached out for its own colors, and a committee consisting of W. H. Slack and Clarence Moore was appointed for the purpose of making a selection. While reviewing the history of the wearing of scarlet in the hunting field in this country they came upon the Washington Hunt, of which the M.F.H. had been Sir Charles Vaughan, the British Minister, who was also a member of the Warwickshire Hunt in England. It seems Sir Charles had adopted the colors of the Warwickshire — scarlet and black — for the Washington hunt, and when it ceased to exist the colors went into mothballs, as it were, until the committee deemed it proper that they should be revived for Chevy Chase.

Drags vs. Live Fox Chases

Theodore Roosevelt in his *Cross Country Riding in America*, writes:

> Of course, the men who ride hard and straight should form the nucleus of every hunt; yet they should be only a fraction of those who come to the meets, for the chief charm of the sport is that almost every man who rides at all can, if he chooses, enjoy it after his own fashion. As most men are not men of means who can afford to devote their whole time to pleasure, the majority are obliged to accommodate their sports to their more serious occupations. The only way to insure this is to have a drag hunt, in which the beginning and the end can be reasonably determined.

A single ride after a drag across country will yield more exercise, fun and excitement, than can be got out of a week's decorous and dull riding in the park, and a majority of the Chevy Chase riders had undoubtedly waked up to this fact. This was true of the Meadowbrook, the Myopia and a great many other hunt clubs, where nine out of ten runs were after a drag. In all this enthusiasm the sport at Chevy Chase had developed a tendency to become more and more like a steeplechase (speed never bothered the Chevy Chase set) in which none but the very best horses, mainly thoroughbreds, could take part, and while they can do more with less effort and fatigue than any other breed, they are the hardest to ride.

On the other hand, for men who have the time and inclination, men who thrill to the hesitant note of a hound feathering on a cold trail, nothing can take the place of the chase of a live fox. It is not only a hazardous adventure, but for the initiated, despite its time-consuming proclivities, it is a savage, unpredictable struggle against a sly, resourceful quarry which can and does put the most skilled of huntsmen and the hardiest of hounds on their mettle. Like what Grandma said about making apple pie — first get your apples — in fox hunting it's first find your fox, which means you never know when the real chase will begin, how long it will last, or where it will end.

The Charms of A Fox Hunt

There are few more delightful experiences in every way than to go out with hounds early in the morning. If the meet is at daybreak, the field is small and wholly made up of those who really love the sport. You ride away from the kennels in the gray dawn, everything is still and perhaps a thin mist hangs over the pastures. When the covert is reached, the hounds are thrown in, and there can be no prettier sight than to see them working over the damp ground where scent is sure to lie well. The air bites a little, the horses are at their best, and nothing can be more exhilarating or more full of healthy and honest pleasure.

The fox hunt to many horsemen, takes the edge off the drag. The fox knows very well what is best for him. He slips along the edges of the woods, plunges into a dense thicket, comes out on the other side, skirts the covert again, finally crosses a swamp and very probably escapes. Now and then he will break from one covert to another; sometimes he takes boldly to the open and then comes the best of all things — a sharp run on a burning scent.

Fox hunting requires nerve, courage and skill, and no sport demanding these qualities can be foreign to an American. Nothing can be more false than the idea that cross country riding is the amusement of the very rich and the very exclusive. It is the most democratic, as it is the best, field sport in the world.

A Fast Drag

I remember a very delightful drag with the Chevy Chase Hounds, in which I had the honor of riding one of the best horses in Mr. Moore's stable. We started from where the fire house now stands on Connecticut Avenue, just south of Chevy Chase Lake. The course followed the trail of an imaginary fox and was laid by a rider dragging a fox-hide or a sack of anise seed, to simulate the course Reynard would take if and when hounds got on his trail. After allowing the drag man a ten-minute leeway, Mr. Moore gave the word and Bob Curran and his Whips, who have the drag pack out, lead hounds into the field where they soon picked up the scent. We followed across Brookeville Road, the entire pack in full chorus and the excited riders taking fences and ditches in stride, many of the barriers being stone walls and those old snake, or zigzag fences you rarely see any more. Swinging to the right we splashed through the ford, crossing Rock Creek at what is now the foot of Leland Street, thence north on the meadows skirting the creek, to a colored settlement called Monkey Hollow, everybody rushing out and cheering us. It was a fast thing on to the bare farmlands south of the Kensington-Wheaton road, the chase eventually pulling up (hunters call it a "check") where the drag had been lifted near a big gum tree in Wheaton. Bob Curran had his hounds well in hand at the end of the seven mile chase, for the scent had run out and the drag man was some quarter of a mile to the west, mounting his horse to plot the return run. All the riders had dismounted to give their horses a breather and tighten girths. Then the drag man disappeared and we knew it was time to get in the saddle again.

Hound Music Heard

Pretty soon we heard Curran's horn tooting the hounds away. They responded by a crash of music and we pressed our mounts for the second lap. I can best describe my feelings as ecstatic; I had never ridden a horse like Lord Craven — the grandest hunter I had ever thrown a leg over; he was a lean rangy bay, with a mouth like velvet and entirely responsive to my every signal. He jumped his fences boldly, standing well back as he took off, and landing like a feather. Eventually we came to a high bluff overlooking Rock Creek Valley, hounds delirious and every person riding like mad, Mr. Moore up front with the Huntsman and Whippers-in and some fifty feet to the rear of the racing pack. "Sit well back," Mr. Moore shouted as we approached down hill to a ragged stone wall, "there's water and a big drop on the other side." His warning saved us all, for it was a blind, tricky hazard.

The Master Comes a Cropper

Nevertheless, the M. F. H., riding the veteran hunter, Red Fox, came a cropper in the icy stream. He rose in water to his waist, blew the mud from his mouth and scrambled out. Red Fox was quickly caught and the Master remounted, the drag eventually hauling up on George Dunlop's estate, Hayes Manor. Mr. Dunlop had plenty of refreshments and a cheery fire going in his library and Mr. Moore was soon dried out. Memory at times is fickle, so I will not attempt to recall the dozen or more who rode in the hunt; yet I have a distinct recollection of Miss Frances Moore, daughter of the M. F. H., steering her clever black mare, Miss Lenah, side saddle.

Hunting continued through the fall and winter. Among numerous meets we note those at the Club and at "Woodley", the residence of Mr. and Mrs. Charles H. L. Johnston; at Mr. Gist Blair's place in Silver Spring, fox hunts at Cabin John's Bridge and Potomac, and drags from the Tennallytown Power House and from the Ray farm on Brookeville Road. In the latter, Mr. Martin of the German Embassy got a severe fall. The Post of January 22, 1905, gives this report of the run:

Chevy Chase Hunt Club Has An Exciting
Ten-Mile Run

The Chevy Chase Hounds met yesterday at the Ray farm, where at 3:30 the pack started up the heights and across the B. & O. Railroad to Forest Glen, where the first cast was made on top of the hill. Thence the drag lay south to Linden, where it doubled back northeast to the Reily farm and across the Seventh Street road to the eastern portion of this same property. Here the jumps came thick and fast, and by the time the field had swung round in a complete circle and again crossed the Seventh Street road no less than twelve big fences had been taken.

Through the western portion of the Reily farm the hounds swung north over several jumps, including a difficult "in and out" across the Forest Glen road, where they turned northwest to Capital View. At that point a "walking check" took place, and upon reaching the heights on the west side of the Baltimore and Ohio Railway the pack was again thrown in; through the woods ran the hounds, across the brook, which was barred by a very "trappy" rail fence, to the Ray farm, where hounds turned south over the stone wall to the broad meadows, and describing a semi-circle, which carried the field over a big slat fence, continued across the Kensington trolley line. Here the pack turned sharply north, then west over a brook, northwest over a barred jump, and west over a big post and rail fence into the woods.

Mr. Martin's Horse Falls

At North Chevy Chase the drag lay along the Kensington Road to the Jones Mill Road, but upon reaching the Dunlop farm it turned south across that property to the woods. A jump carried the field into the Klein farm, where Mr. Martin got a bad fall. The hounds continued by an in-and-out jump across a road into the Bean place, and again swinging southeast, ran through the woods and the Watkins farm to the finish, opposite the Chevy

19

Chase Inn, a half mile north of the Chevy Chase Club.

In spite of the heavy going no less than ten miles were covered at a lively pace and thirty-one fences encountered. It was an exceptionally good run for any pack.

Among those who followed were Mrs. Charles H. L. Johnston, Mrs. Preston Gibson, Miss Gaff, Miss Field, Mr. Frederic L. Huidekoper, acting master of hounds; Mr. Martin of the German Embassy; Capt. Langhorne, Mr. Reginald Huidekoper, Mr. Marshall Langhorne, Mr. Charles H. L. Johnston, and Mr. Chester Kerr.

The huntsman, Robert Curran, was mounted on Masterpiece, and the Whip, George Curran, on a gray hunter belonging to the Prince de Bearn.

The final run for the season occurred on March 29, 1905, when the hounds met at the Club Kennels at 3:30 o'clock. We are indebted to the Post for a breezy account of the occasion:

Chevy Chase Hunters Have Final Cross-Country Run of Season

Miss Roosevelt at the Clubhouse, Where the Run was Concluded—Large Number Follow Hounds

The hunting season of 1904-1905 in Washington ended yesterday when the Chevy Chase Hounds met at the club kennels at 3:30 o'clock, the start being witnessed by quite a crowd of members.

The pack was thrown in on the east side of Connecticut Avenue, and took a line directly north across the Chevy Chase Land Company's property to the Anderson farm. Bearing thence toward the northwest the hounds crossed the Brookeville road, and, running through the George Dunlop farm to its northern extremity, turned sharply to the west past the power-house across Connecticut Avenue. Beyond the Laird farm the drag lay through some troublesome woods to the south, but emerged at the Klein farm, and circling again to the south came out at the Laird Lane, which was followed as far as Woodmont, where the first walking check was made.

Continuing toward the west, the hounds were again cast at the edge of the Denton farm, and, running through the woods on the south, emerged at the Goldsborough place, only to swing toward the west into the Hardy place, where a nasty Liverpool jump was met, and thence to the north into the Naylor farm. After a lively gallop through the scattering woods the drag circled toward the northeast along the western boundary of the Naylor property, and, doubling back over a snake fence, bore toward the south past the farmhouse, which is surrounded by fences, to the brook beyond. At this point the hounds turned southeast through the woods to the Hardy farm once more, only to double back across the River road into the

the Stack place. At the farther end of this property the drag bore away to the southwest over a succession of jumps, and, swinging directly east over several plowed fields, continued through the Willett place and the Goldsborough farm to West Chevy Chase. After a short check the pack crossed the Rockville road and followed the bridle path along the western edge of the golf links to a finish near the thirteenth hole.

In all eleven miles were covered and more than thirty-five jumps taken. The pace varied greatly, due perhaps to the high temperature, and there were some refusals; but only one fall, which did not prove serious. Among those who followed were Mrs. Arthur Snyder, Miss Elkins, Miss Gaff, Miss Bell, Mr. Frederic Huidekoper, acting master of hounds; Mr. Grip, the Swedish Minister; Count Wenckheim, and Mr. Zichy, of the Austrian Embassy; Mr. Reginald Huidekoper, Capt. Wallach, Mr. Marshall Langhorne, Mr. Charles Johnston, Mr. Albert Carroll, Lt. Montgomery, and a number of others.

The huntsman, Robert Curran, was mounted on Masterpiece, and the Whip, George Curran, on Lady Teazle.

A number of well-known people gathered at the club after the hunt, including Miss Alice Roosevelt.

The Chevy Chase Steeplechase

"I will drink both to thee and thy horse; so courage, frolic; God save the Company."—Rabelais.

In the golden era of the Hunt, the members were a merry, challenging, horse-proud lot, and after the hunting season was over, good natured arguments and sizeable wagers occurred as to who owned the animal with the most speed and stamina. To settle the matter the Washington Jockey Club, operators of the Bennings Race Track, at their regular spring meeting put on a really rugged race, which they called the Chevy Chase Steeplechase. Samuel S. Howland, secretary of the National Hunt and Steeplechase Association, with H. Rozier Dulany and Ben Hellen, controlled the Jockey Club with Algernon Daingerfield as Secretary. The Washington office of the Jockey Club was in the Barton Hotel, site of the Hibbs Building on Fifteenth Street, and Mr. Daingerfield was generous in issuing passes for the races.

It was my good fortune to witness several of these steeplechases, the conditions being that the distance was to be two and a half miles, with fifteen jumps, that only horses which had been hunted with the Chevy Chase Hounds were eligible, as certified by the M. F. H., and that none but "gentlemen" riders would be allowed, the word "gentlemen" distinguishing amateur riders from professional jockeys.

My memory fails to reveal the year that the most outlandish of these hunt steeplechases occurred; anyhow it was a honey, a high mark of the general jollifications that marked some of the races. Sargeant Prentiss Knut, a tall, thin fellow from Natchez, Miss., and one of the "first flight" men at Chevy Chase, owned a flashy bay named Twilight, with docked tail and mouth of iron. Bookmakers, who knew the wild unpredictable nature of the horse, offered fantastic odds on Twilight and Mr. Knut, one handicapper sneeringly writing that it would be "midnight before Twilight finished." When the Southerner heard that remark his blood boiled, and he had a friend bet $20 for him that he would win.

As the horses approached the starter Twilight bolted. Mr. Knut couldn't do a thing with him; he leaped from the infield onto the track, raced there at breakneck speed for several furlongs and then jumped back into the infield, the crowd yelling "Take him off, take him off."

Finally the grim, determined Knut got his horse to the starter. Down went the flag and the horses rushed off on their gruelling journey. The second time around Freddy Huidekoper's horse fell at the water jump in front of the grandstand; a woman shrieked "Goody, goody," and a man yelled "Here's a cake of soap, Freddy." Coming into the home stretch Twilight was running third, and after gradually disposing of the leaders he went on to win amidst wild cheers of the spectators, for Mr. Knut and his comedian of a horse had put on a show the like of which they were never to see again.

"Where's the fellow who said we wouldn't finish before midnight?" drawled the now smiling Knut as he unsaddled Twilight. "I like to jolt a smart Alec and at the same time collect a nice piece of silver—and a juicy bet. Rather sporting, wouldn't you say?"

11,000 See Race

One of the best attended of these Chevy Chase Steeplechases—that of March 28, 1903—drew a large, representative field of riders and a crowd of 11,000, the latter a great outpouring for the Bennings track. In the Club House, Miss Alice Roosevelt and a host of notables witnessed the "leppers" fighting it out, and also the presentation of the trophies, Dion Kerr on Joe Leiter taking first prize—a solid silver punch bowl; John Larcombe, riding his good Jacobel, accounting for the second trophy—a silver riding crop, and Percy Evans on Royal Star, in third place, receiving a pair of silver spurs. The others finished in the following order:

HORSE	RIDER
Hawke	Mr. R. S. Huidekoper
Little Duchess	Mr. Rogers
Kalorama	Mr. F. L. Huidekoper
Rooster	Mr. Spencer
Twilight	Mr. Knut
Dragoman	Mr. Watters

Less than a month later, the winning horse, then at the peak of his fame, met his Waterloo.

Joe Leiter Killed In Race

The Famous Hunter runs His last Steeplechase at Pimlico

Special to Washington Post.

Baltimore, Md., April 23 — The career of Joe Leiter, the famous hunter owned by Dr. James Kerr, of Washington, D. C., was ended in the Carrollton Cup Steeplechase here today. Dr. Kerr's son, Dion Kerr, had the mount, and the horse had taken all the jumps successfully, but just as he challenged Beau Ideal in the final rush on the flat Joe Leiter stumbled and fell. Young Kerr was not hurt and was up in a second, but the horse tore a terrible gash in his chest, and after getting up and dashing riderless past the grandstand, fell dead. Dr. Kerr and his son felt keenly the sad fate of their favorite. Joe Leiter was a bay gelding by Baggage-AusterNelle, and was the best of the qualified hunter class in the South. He won the Chevy Chase Hunt Steeplechase and Southern Hunt Steeplechase at Bennings and the Elkridge Hunt Steeplechase at Pimlico this spring.

Dion Kerr

At that period, when he was around twenty, Dion's mother was not keen on his riding in races, especially steeplechases, an opinion not shared by his sportsman father. As fate decreed, the lion hearted Dion (brother of our Dr. Harry Kerr), in spite of numerous accidents (he said he was all wired up inside), recovered from them all and lived to be seventy-two.

If I were asked who was the leading gentleman rider in the thrilling and risky sport of racing at speed over obstacles, I would answer, Dion Kerr, without a doubt. No man ever had a greater love for a good horse. He used to say, "You can do what you want with a horse until fifty yards from a jump, but after that you must leave him alone."

Many are the good races I have seen Dion ride and I can hardly recall ever seeing him ride a bad one, which I could not say of any other rider, professional or amateur. Dion was up to every trick in the trade and at the same time he was the fairest rider that ever got into a saddle. Later he trained horses, the greatest of which was Aneroid, winner of many high class stake races, one time beating the redoubtable Seabiscuit.

Smart Set On Hand

Now I will tell of the 1905 race. On that Saturday of late March the fickle goddess, Nature, was in one of her happy moods and the first touch of spring was in the air. The clubhouse enclosure was filled with the smart set from New York, Washington, and nearby cities, and there were few vacant seats in the grandstand. The weights the horses were to carry were publicly announced and the following letter was sent to Bob Curran:

Metropolitan Club
Washington, D. C.
March 21, 1905

At a meeting of the Stewards of the Washington Jockey Club today it was decided that Montrip will carry 168 pounds; Sifter 160; Twilight 158; Jacobel 150; Duke of Grasslands 150; Dragoman 148; Rooster 148; Follow On 147.

I saw Mr. Percy Evans today and he assured me his brother would certainly ride Montrip.

I shall probably be unable to hunt tomorrow but want you again to give a mount to Mr. Wallach. You may select the horse.

Yours truly,
Frederic L. Huidekoper

As usual the conditions were that the riders must wear hunting pink coat and high silk hat, or black velvet hunting cap, at the option of the rider. This gave the race a spectacular effect and added to its attractiveness. There were six starters: Clarence Moore's Montrip, ridden by Lee Evans of the Warrenton Hunt; A. B. Langhorne's Sifter, ridden by Fred Okie of the Meadowbrook; Prentiss Knut's Twilight, ridden by the owner; Mr. Knut's other entry, Duke of Grasslands, ridden by Mr. Parsons of the Deep Run Hunt (Va.); John Larcombe's Jacobel, ridden by Dion Kerr of the Warrenton Hunt; A. A. Snyder's Rooster, ridden by Jervis Spencer of the Green Spring Valley Hunt.

The Betting Odds

Naturally there was considerable speculation on the contest as it had attracted cross country enthusiasts from many sections, and not without cause, for the race had the spectators on their toes from start to finish. Each rider had a strong following regardless of his mount, and a large sum of money was wagered with the bookmakers. The heavy play was on Sifter, who was backed down to 5 to 2. Montrip, the top weight, moved from 5 to 2 to 4 to 1, and Jacobel was always around 4 to 1. Mr. Knut's entry, Twilight and Duke of Grasslands, were quoted at 2 to 1 at starting time. Rooster, the long shot, was 15 to 1.

As the horses and their scarlet clad riders came from the paddock they made a lovely picture and were lustily cheered. When they entered the infield the fun began. Old Twilight, erratic as usual, began prancing around and Mr. Knut's silk hat fell off. The other riders apparently concluded the headgear was intended only for the parade, and the line of march to the starter was strewn with silk hats and velvet caps.

Twilight Throws Mr. Knut

Mars Cassidy, the starter, gave the signal and the horses went to the first jump pretty well strung out. Twilight, one of the leaders, fumbled the barrier and threw Mr. Knut heavily to the ground, the horse apparently rolling over the prostrate form of the rider. He was quickly attended, however, by the officers and physicians, and the crowd, which was momentarily shocked, again directed its attention to the contest. Duke of Grasslands jumped into the lead but held it only a short time when he ran out, the real race being between Jacobel and Montrip for the first half of the journey. They see-sawed for the lead, with Sifter always in striking distance. When the fence which brought Twilight to grief was taken the second time, Mr. Okie on Sifter gave an exhibition of jockeyship that earned him a round of applause. Sifter, making a bad landing, threw his rider out of the saddle, but Mr. Okie clung tenaciously to his mount and righted himself quickly, Sifter losing little ground.

Rooster in Trouble

Meanwhile Lee Evans, who was riding a brilliant race on Montrip, finally shook off Jacobel after jumping the last fence, where Rooster fell with Mr. Spencer, who remounted and continued. No sooner had Montrip got rid of one contender than trouble came from another quarter. Mr. Okie got busy on Sifter and was fast gaining on the leader entering the stretch. Mr. Evans realized that it was do or die; Sifter was showing no signs of weakening and in a few more strides Lee Evans went to the bat and the steel and catgut fell on the silken flanks of Montrip. In the last hundred yards it was a furious drive, both riders whipping desperately and their mounts all-out with everything they had. But Sifter could never get up to the big brown horse, and Montrip won by half a length. Sifter was second, Jacobel third, with the game Mr. Spencer fourth on Rooster.

This was the fourth running of the Chevy Chase and the best contest it had produced. Mr. Okie, for his sensational recovery from what looked like a certain spill, and Mr. Spencer, for his plucky half-mile ride with a broken collarbone which he had sustained when Rooster fell, shared the honors with Mr. Evans, who handled Montrip in faultless style. Clarence Moore was not at home and did not have the pleasure of seeing Montrip's victory. However, Bob Curran, his trainer, was on hand. The Chevy Chase prize was all in plate, a piece going to each of the first three horses.

Going back to 1902, the race that year was won by J. Van Ness Phillip's Hari Kiri, ridden by the owner; in 1903 by Dion Kerr piloting Joe Leiter as mentioned above, and Sargeant Prentiss Knut on Twilight gathered the laurels in 1904, but this was an evenly run race and not the erratic one previously described.

Comment on the Race

In the paddock after Montrip's victory, there were various and sundry opinions on the running of the race. Jimmy Johnson, the trainer of Sifter, was sure he had sent the best horse to the post. He thought Sifter lost because of his blunders, which in turn were due to the unsafe state of the going. "We should have won this race sure," declared Johnson, vehemently, "and if Mr. Clarence Moore does not think so, tell him I will meet him at any time at $500 a side, the horses to run the same distance they covered today under the same weight and riders."

Mara Says He Did It

Jimmie Mara, well-known Socrates of the racing world, took unto himself full credit for Montrip's victory. "It was not the horse and it was not the rider," Jimmie declared cryptically, "although I have to own up that they done well. Montrip jumped better than he ever jumped before, and Mr. Evans sat on him like a man glued on. But I did it all. I like to encourage these young gentlemen riders, and I have noticed that Mr. Evans has a way of thinking he is through after going a mile. So I told him to recollect that he was in a two mile and a half, and not pull up after the first round of the field. He obeyed my instructions to the letter. If he'll only listen to me I'll make a steeplechase rider out of him yet."

Meanwhile, the exuberant fans who had backed Montrip trooped up to the bookmakers and cleared a juicy $40 for every $10 they had wagered.

Winner Take All

Once horses get into your blood the malady is practically incurable. You breed them, race them, play polo, hunt them, show them—or merely go hacking in the park. So it was at Chevy Chase in "the old days", and now that we have had a fling at hunting and racing we can look in on a show or two.

Mr. Moore who generally spent the summers with his family at Swiftmoor, their country place at Prides Crossing, Massachusetts, competed in shows at Newport, Myopia Hunt and elsewhere. It was at Newport that our M. F. H., to settle a friendly argument, pitted Koohinoor, his big 16 hands two inches show jumper, against the other gentleman's Mr. Jorrocks, the winning owner to take the losing animal—a sporting horse for horse battle. Ridden by Bob Curran, Koohinoor did everything that was asked of him, finally beating his opponent when the bars got high enough, and Mr. Moore acquired Mr. Jorrocks.

High Jump At Rockville Fair

Each summer the Rockville Fair was a popular gathering place for Montgomery County folk. There were hound and horse, hog and cattle exhibits, races and jumping contests, speeches by local politicians and the inevitable brass band. In the farm women's pavilion one could see ornate displays of home products, canned vegetables and peach and pear preserves. For farmers and their women folk the Fair was a whoop-la.

One day Bob Curran took it into his head to ride to the Fair with his two Whips, all three in full hunting regalia, in order to add a little sporting zip to the proceedings. When the high jumping contest was announced, Bob entered Masterpiece and was so successful that he broke the record for height, winning an enormous silver trophy. Bob was afraid to tell the M. F. H. of his triumph, but the boss somehow learned about it. Sternly rebuking Bob for risking Masterpiece in such a severe test, he declared if Bob did such a thing again he would have the horse put down.

A Show For Charity

One sunny spring day as the dogwood blossomed and the robins carolled, the members of the Hunt and the 7th U. S. Cavalry put on a show for the benefit of "charity, sweet charity". We are able to give the first page of the program:

JUMPING COMPETITION FOR HUNTERS

in connection with the

GARDEN PARTY

for the benefit of

THE WASHINGTON HOME FOR INCURABLES

to be held at

"FRIENDSHIP"

the country residence of

JOHN R. McLEAN, ESQ.

SATURDAY, MAY SIXTH, 1905
at three p. m.

*   *   *

FREDERIC L. HUIDEKOPER
Captain ROBERT R. WALLACH
M. MARSHALL LANGHORNE
Horse Show Committee

For an excellent description of the event we are indebted to The Star of May 7, 1905, which said:

Blooded Hunters Compete at Society Garden Party

"The garden party yesterday at Friendship was a tremendous success and the great crescent formed around the lawn to watch the hunter competition and the trooper's drill was an inspiring sight and one not possible to frequently reproduce. The list of names, if printed, would suggest diplomatic night at the White House. The Marine Band played in the south garden and each visitor was free to enjoy every inch of the drawing room floor, the living room, billiard room, and verandas, as well as the gardens about the mansion, the tennis courts, shady walks and fine roads that lead from point to point.

"For nearly three hours the spectators watched with close attention the hunter's contest and the competitive fancy riding of the 7th United States Cavalry. The chief judge was Courtland H. Smith of Alexandria, with Ned McLean and Colonel Robert Neville as assistants. Granville R. Fortescue served as the official starter. The ribbons were given the winners of the same on the field, but the prizes were presented at the conclusion of the exercises by Mr. Fortescue in the McLean residence. First prize in each event was a silver cup valued at $50, and second prize was a silver cup valued at $35.

"In Class 1, the opening event, were heavy-weight hunters carrying up to 185 pounds to hounds. Miss Newland's Rajah was ridden by Capt. Robert R. Wallach, Mr. Clarence Moore's Cardinal by Mr. Frederic Huidekoper, Mr. Clarence Moore's Masterpiece by Mr. Reginald Huidekoper, Mr. Pierre Lorillard's Czardas by Mr. H. L. Ewart of the British Embassy, and Mr. C. H. L. Johnston's Red Gauntlet by the owner.

"The blue ribbon, denoting first place, was awarded to Mr. Reginald Huidekoper, who, as stated, rode Masterpiece; the red ribbon, denoting second place, to Capt. Wallach, who rode Rajah, and the yellow ribbon, denoting third place, to Mr. Ewart, who rode Czardas. First prize was donated by Mr. T. T. Gaff, and second prize by Mr. Charles J. Bell.

Middle and Lightweight Hunters

"The second event, Class 2, was open to middle and lightweight hunters. Mrs. Preston Gibson's Lois Huntington was ridden by the owner; Miss Field's Chappie Lee was ridden by the owner; Miss Gaff's Blazeway, by Capt. Wallach; Mr. Clarence Moore's Charles O'Malley, by Mr. Frederic Huidekoper; Mr. Frederic Huidekoper's Mantahala, by the owner, Mr. Reginald Huidekoper's Pontiac, by the owner; Mr. Roger Wetmore's La Touraine and his Little Duchess, both by Mr. Chester Carr; Mr. C. H. L. Johnston's Devil-to-Get, by Mrs. Johnston; Mr. John Merriam's Mr. Dooley, by Mr. Chester Carr; Dr. A. A. Snyder's

Rooster, by the owner; Mr. R. Lewis' Buckskin, by the
the owner, and Cerro, a cavalry troop horse, by Capt.
Wallach. Capt. Wallach and Mrs. Gibson were tied for
first place and therefore they took an additional try at
the fences. The blue rbibon was finally awarded to Capt.
Wallach and Cerro, amid the tumultuous applause of the
Fort Myer cavalrymen. The red ribbon went to Mrs.
Preston Gibson and her Lois Huntington, and the yellow
ribbon to Mr. Frederic Huidekoper and Mr. Moore's
Charles O'Malley. First prize was donated by Mr. G. Loth-
rop Bradley, and second prize by Mr. William Reyburn.
Mr. Dooley refused three times to take the jump, and
was ruled out of the running.

The Third Event

"After general hurdle jumping by all the cavalrymen
in attendance the third event was called. It was a fancy
riding contest, without saddles, by squads of six men
each from Troops C, D and A, 7th United States Cavalry,
for silver cup prizes donated by Mr. Pierre Lorillard
and Mr. William P. Eno. The men and horses took the
fences singly, doubly and in all imaginable ways, including the entire squads formed as pyramids on the
horses. The exhibition was a spectacular one and aroused
much enthusiasm, especially among the soldier spectators. The fact that the drill of each squad was limited
to six minutes hurried and handicapped the troopers and
marred their work to a considerable extent. Major Beach
of the War Department general staff, who judged the
contest, awarded first prize to the squad in charge of
Sargeant Young, from Troop C; second prize to the squad
in charge of Sergeant Burnett, representing Troop D, and
third prize to the squad in charge of Corporal Hadden,
representing Troop A.
"Following the cavalry contest was Class 3 of the
jumping competitions, open to ladies' hunters, ridden by
the ladies. Mrs. Gibson's Lois Huntington was ridden by
the owner; Miss Field's Chappie Lee, by the owner; Miss
Newlands' Rajah, by Mrs. C. H. L. Johnston; Miss Gaff's
Blazeaway, by the owner; Mr. C. H. L. Johnston's Devil-
to-Get, by Mrs. Johnston, and Dr. A. A. Snyder's Rooster,
by Miss Field. Miss Gaff sustained a bad fall at the first
barrier, but pluckily announced that she intended to resume riding. A broken pommel on her saddle, however,
compelled her to desist. Mrs. Gibson and her sister,
Miss Field, on Rooster, were tied for first place, so they
rode again. The blue ribbon was earned by Miss Field and
"Rooster"; the red ribbon by Mrs. Gibson, and the yellow
ribbon by Miss Field and "Chappie Lee". First prize was
donated by Mrs. Oliver Cromwell and second prize by
Mrs. Arthur Lee.

Open to All Hunters

"The concluding event, Class 4, was open to all hunters. Mrs. Gibson's Lois Huntington was ridden by the

owner; Miss Field's Chappie Lee, by the owner; Mr. Moore's Masterpiece, by Mr. Reginald Huidekoper; Mr. Moore's Charles O'Malley, by Mr. Frederic Huidekoper; Mr. Lorillard's Czardas, by Mr. Ewart; Mr. R. Huidekoper's Pontiac, by the owner; Mr. Johnston's Red Gauntlet, by the owner; Mr. Merriam's Mr. Dooley, by Mr. Chester Carr; Mr. Wetmore's Little Duchess, by Mr. Carr, and Cerro, by Captain Wallach. Mr. Frederic Huidekoper sustained a fall at the second fence, but promptly mounted and finished the course. For the second time during the afternoon Mr. Dooley positively refused thrice to take the jump, and was not considered in the reckoning. The blue ribbon was awarded to Mr. Reginald Huidekoper and "Masterpiece"; the red ribbon to Mrs. Gibson, and the yellow ribbon, which seemed to be entirely appropriate, even though it meant third place, for a cavalry officer and a cavalry horse, to Captain Wallach and "Cerro". First prize was donated by Mr. Larz Anderson and second prize by Mr. Gist Blair."

A Big Letdown

The criticism about the hunts being too social, mostly drags, and possibly differences of opinion within the club could have touched the M. F. H. in a tender spot, and in his dilemma he turned to Virginia with her sporting horse breeders and master race riders—Jim Maddux, "Courty" Smith, Lee Evans, Dick Wallach, Jim Skinner, Louis Leith and some Englishmen of the right sort for that kind of rollicking life—fox hunting, point to point steeplechasing, cock fighting and all that. At that period and later, as will be revealed, the Old Dominion seemed to hold an irresistible attraction for Clarence Moore, who probably felt the futility of trying to please everybody at Chevy Chase, and in the summer of 1905 he moved his horses and the hounds (which were his property), as well as the Staff to Warrenton, occupying a farm near Dick Wallach's place and naming a fine bay horse, Little Dick, after him. There is a fleeting hint of friction between the hunt and the Club for on September 1, 1905, "Robert Curran, Manager, of the Chevy Chase Club Stables" billed the Club for "Manure left, about 50 loads, $25.00". During Mr. Moore's absence things naturally looked discouraging. It was a big letdown. But Gist Blair and Charles H. L. Johnston carried on in the awkward circumstances and showed fair sport with such American hounds as they could get together. (I remember seeing Mr. Blair riding his Maryland in one of the Hunt Steeplechases.)

The English-American Fox Hound Match

While in Virginia Mr. Moore undoubtedly witnessed the famous English-American fox hound match, which, following years of heated arguments, took place in the Piedmont Valley in November, 1905. The masters of 26 hunts were present with advocates on both sides of the controversy. The main difference, briefly, is that in hunting an American pack the huntsman allows hounds to hunt the fox and follows them wherever they go, rarely interfering in any way, while in England the fox—in a sense—is hunted by the huntsman, who instantly goes to the assistance of his hounds when difficulties arise. Entered against the Grafton Hounds, a home bred American pack owned by Harry Worcester Smith, M. F. H., were the Middlesex Fox Hounds, a draft English pack, the property of A. Henry Higginson, M. F. H. Neither pack succeeded in killing a fox during several days of hunting, and while the American hounds were awarded a rather hollow victory, neither Mr. Smith nor Mr. Higginson altered his opinion as to the relative merits of the two types. (It should be stated, however, for the record that the Middlesex did kill a fox, but since the judges considered it to have been chopped in covert the kill was not scored.)

Hunting Humor and 'Ware Holes'

In that erudite and monumental volume "Hunting in The United States and Canada", by Alex Higginson and Julian Chamberlain, there is this amusing story about English hounds:

> For years there had been many arguments about the merits of English and American hounds. The former were considered by many to be unfit for our country as being too heavy and slow in getting through the bush and over the walls and fences. On the other hand, it was claimed for American hounds, somewhat lighter than the English and showing more quality than size and substance, that while they were harder to control in the field, they really rattled their fox along in a hard driving way and were able to recover a lost line quicker than the hounds from the other side; also that American hounds gave tongue more freely, which to many hunters is a most desirable quality. Down in Virginia on a certain occasion after the English pack of the local hunt had been roundly abused the evening before, as not being able to hunt the country satisfactorily, the hunt went out the following morning and when the hounds were cast they went straight off with noses to ground and giving tongue at every stride. There was a marvellous run for some ten miles over level turf, but the hounds lost at the end and to every ones astonishment not a single hound was able to recover the line. The fox had escaped in a mysterious fashion; so all hands went home, a tired but enthusiastic lot. Sometime later they discovered that it was all a hoax. A drag had been laid by a facetious fellow over a country which the English hounds could negotiate.

And of long winter evenings, sitting by the fire in the Fauquier Club of Warrenton, gathering place for the sporting crew, Mr. Moore could have heard "Courty" Smith reciting "The Gent From London Way", otherwise known as "Ware Holes", a great favorite with hunting men:

'WARE HOLES!

By Arthur Conan Doyle

['Ware Holes!' is the expression used in the hunting field to warn those behind against rabbit-burrows or other such dangers]

A sportin' death! My word it was!
   An' taken in a sportin' way.
Mind you, I wasn't there to see;
   I only tell you what they say.

They found that day at Shillinglee,
  An' ran 'im down to Chillinghurst;
The fox was goin' straight an' free
  For ninety minutes at a burst.

They 'ad a check at Ebernoe
  An' made a cast across the Down,
Until they got a view 'ullo
  An' chased 'im up to Kirdford town.

From Kirdford 'e run Bramber way,
  An' took 'em over 'alf the weald.
If you'ave tried the Sussex clay,
  You'll guess it weeded out the field.

Until at last I don't suppose
  As 'arf a dozen, at the most,
Came safe to where the grassland goes
  Switchbackin' southwards to the coast.

Young Captain 'Eadley, 'e was there,
  And Jim the whip an' Percy Day;
The Purcells an' Sir Charles Adair,
  An' this 'ere gent from London way.

For 'e 'ad gone amazin' fine,
  Two 'undred pounds* between 'is knees;
Eight stone he was, an' rode at nine,
  As light an' limber as you please,

'E was a stranger to the 'Unt,
  There weren't a person as 'e knew there;
But 'e could ride, that London gent—
  'E sat 'is mare as if 'e grew there.

They seed the 'ounds upon the scent,
  But found a fence across their track,
And 'ad to fly it; else it meant
  A turnin' and a 'arkin' back.

'E was the foremost at the fence,
  And as 'is mare just cleared the rail
'E turned to them that rode be'ind
  For three was at 'is very tail.

'Ware 'oles!' says 'e, an' with the word,
  Still sittin' easy on his mare,
Down, down 'e went, an' down an' down,
  Into the quarry yawin' there.

Some say it was two 'undred foot;
  The bottom lay as black as ink.
I guess they 'ad some ugly dreams,
  Who reined their 'orses on the brink.

'E'd only time for that one cry;
  'Ware 'oles!' says 'e, an' saves all three.
There may be better deaths to die,
  But that one's good enough for me.

31

For mind you, 'twas a sportin' end,
    Upon a right good sportin' day;
They think a deal of 'im down 'ere,
    That gent what came from London way."

*Value of the horse

Complaints in the Village

With the rise of the Chevy Chase as a golf club, the golfing members displayed a growing tendency not to contribute to the hunt in which they never rode. Moreover, the Villagers began to complain about the baying of the hounds, and after the hunting and racing were over in the spring of 1906, the Board of Governors voted not to continue the subscription to the pack and such hounds as were on hand were taken to an estate near Chevy Chase Lake. However, the Board was merely expressing its dissatisfaction with the handling of the hunt by the acting M. F. H., Charles H. L. Johnston, a friendly fellow who never seemed to grow up, and had in mind at that time of persuading Clarence Moore to return. And that is exactly what happened, for come the frost on the pumpkin and hunting in the air, the Board voted to resume the annual subscription and invited Mr. Moore to come back, adding that the hounds should be kenneled at some place other than the Club.

In the autumn of 1906 the Moore hunting entourage returned from the Old Dominion and occupied Rock Creek Farms near Kensington, which Mr. Moore had purchased and where he had built ample stables and kennels, Bob Curran and his family occupying a house already on the property. The M. F. H. seemed to love the farm and nothing gave him more pleasure than to roam over the grassy fields with his dogs and his son Clarence Moore, Jr., accompanied by Joe Curran, the Huntsman's young son, the boys being devoted friends.

Another son, Preston Moore, living in Papeete, Tahiti, French Oceania, writes feelingly to Mr. Lynham about his father and the old days:

> Your letter has released in me a flood of memories, but unfortunately, no papers or photographs. My family has been widely dispersed and I have lived here in Tahiti for well over 25 years and most records of our former life in Washington have been lost. All that I have is a number of silver cups, punch bowls, etc., of the Club, with engravings of the different horseshows and the names of the different hunters who won the prizes, but I doubt if these would interest present members.

> While very young at the time, I well remember the old Clubhouse which was an old clapboard, white-washed farm house with the tack room building off to the left of the main building. My father had a farm farther out where we kept the hunters, sometimes as many as 80 or 90 and anywhere from 2 to 5 packs of hounds. The kennels were quite extensive with a very big kitchen for cooking their food. The exercising and training of these hounds and hunters were a daily occurrence. Sometimes a pack was quartered for a while on the Club's premises when the hunts started from there.

My father started my education in the hunting field quite early and I took part in many hunts. I was given a 7/8 Thoroughbred hunter called Warrenton, where we bred a few hunters and he was quite a handful for a small boy. It was hard training and I had little time to give to the social amenities of the field, but I do remember today the kindness of a Mr. Frederic Huidekoper, an old Washington resident who often helped me in difficult passages. The hunts were hard driving in those days and it took courage and stamina to last out. I can remember starting at dawn and arriving back at 3 in the afternoon after a particularly long and hard chase. I don't remember whether we got the fox that particular time or not, but I still remember that day.

I am very touched that there are still people who are interested in the old Washington and that the Chevy Chase Club honors the memory of my father Clarence Moore. Please believe that I am at your entire service to do anything I possibly can to keep the memory of Clarence Moore alive.

Flair For Clothes

Mr. Moore, a tall, brown-eyed man with a small mustache, an athletic figure and a flair for clothes, dressed sportingly, yet in the best of taste. A perfectionist in many ways, he once had a Whip remove signs of white-wash from his horse's bridle. He rode "long", sitting well back in the saddle, which is the opposite of the modern style—short stirrups and forward seat. In the field, where he was as completely in charge as a captain on his ship, he stood for no infraction of the hunting code, being especially severe on members riding too close on the pack. Singling out the culprit, he would blow his whistle and shout: "Hold hard, there, hold hard; don't overrun the hounds." Normally, however, he was always considerate of the other fellow, be he stable boy, club member, diplomat, or the ancient negro who kept a few skinny hounds in a pen behind his cabin. On his frequent visits to the Huntsman's house, the M. F. H. insisted he be treated as a member of the family, and so it was. In town he lived in a baronial mansion (now the Canadian Embassy) and maintained a large brick stable and carriage house near 22nd and P Streets, N. W. Some folks remember him in top boots, white breeches, pink coat and dark blue cap, driving friends to meets in his red and black four-in-hand coach, with a liveried footman blowing coaching tunes on the long brass horn. Wherever hounds met, his horse would be waiting for him, a sandwich in the leather case, whiskey in the flask, and the little brass horn, all properly attached to the saddle. In conformity with immemorial custom, it was within his sole discretion as Master to grant the coveted privilege of riding in the hunt colors, and when a member sported the "pink", you knew he had proved himself a top flight man to hounds. With his hand always in his pocket, the Master saw to it that no one ever brought a lost hound to the kennels, or helped to keep poachers away from the den where a vixen and her mate were raising their cubs (only one litter a year), without receiving a generous reward, and while he carefully selected his intimates from the ranks of the elite, he was nevertheless recieved as a fellow sportsman by the farming community.

Sporting Farmers

There was sporting blood in these farmers of "Old Montgomery" as they called the county, named after General Richard Montgomery, a hero of the Revolution. Some were flamboyant characters, not intimidated by law or custom. With them hospitality was a religion; Ben Ray, whose house topped a hill overlooking Rock Creek, kept a five gallon demijohn of Maryland rye on his front porch, with a tin cup beckoning all comers. An old farmer who lived near Rockville once rode his horse on the sidewalk going into town and was hailed into court. "Five dollars," said the Judge. "Make it ten", the farmer replied, "because I am going to ride on the sidewalk when I leave town." If the Hunt was gay and joyous, the country folk over whose lands they rode, were equally light hearted, although no one worked harder than the farmers.

Jousting was a summer sport for young gallants, in which the "Knight" on a galloping horse aims to spear a series of small rings hung from poles, the winner having the privilege of crowning his girl the Queen of Love and Beauty at the Tournament Ball. Then there were barbecues, hilarious get togethers at hog killing time, and in the dead of winter all-night coon hunts with those sad-faced black and tan hounds, who had voices deep as thunder. They rode first class horses, these men of the soil, many of them thoroughbreds which they raced at county fairs. They attended cock fights at Phil Steubener's pit in the Palo Alto tavern at Bladensburg; and when the Sheriff wasn't looking Joe Turner, a Georgetown boxing entrepreneur, pulled off prize fights in abandoned barns, the novelty of the evening generally being a "battle royal". This rough and tumble affair called for four colored boxers to take the ring and engage in a free for all slugging match, no blows barred, the man remaining on his feet after the others had been knocked out drawing down the cash prize.

One of the popular horses at County race meets was McFonso, a hardy fellow over a distance of ground. He had never raced against top flight horses and his owner, Frank Keys of Linden, near Kensington, after trying him under a stop watch, decided he was worth a go at Bennings. Accordingly, Frank entered his dark horse in a mile and a quarter race on the flat and backed him to the limit, although his competitors were some of the best horses then racing. Bob Curran, Dion Kerr, John Larcombe, Cy Cummings, Ben Ray and others whom Frank had tipped off, got down bets at fantastic odds.

To the amazement of the general public and consternation of the bookmakers, McFonso, who had been given scant consideration (like a bushleaguer daring a big fellow) won his race and thereby effected quite a redistribution of wealth among the local bourgeoise. To make the story even more thrilling, McFonso broke out of his stall at the track that night and appeared next morning at his home stable. The distance from Bennings to Linden is approximately eighteen miles. When McFonso died, Frank had the old hero buried at Linden and the grave marked by a granite boulder.

Fractious Colts

Up at Rock Creek Farms, where around twenty men were employed, there were mares and foals to be looked after, hounds to be mated, puppies trained, colts broken, and hunters schooled, not to mention the urgent necessity of prompt attendance at hunt fixtures. George Eustis paid $12,000 for a two year old thoroughbred colt which he hoped to race. He sent the bay youngster to the farm and when he arrived Bob Curran and his helpers could not persuade him to enter the barn. Suddenly he changed his mind and bolted into his stall, injuring himself so seriously that he was useless as a racing prospect. "How can I explain this terrible accident to Mr. Eustis; no one at the farm is to blame," said Bob, sadly, "the colt came to us with little or no gentling and we did the best we could." At the same time Mr. Eustis (who took the loss philosophically), had another colt (a chestnut) at the farm and he, too, was so rebellious no one could handle him. On a hot summer day as the men were hauling hay Mr. Eustis arrived and had the colt brought out. The heat and the four horse team inspired an idea. "Put him in as the off lead (right side) horse of the hay wagon", he ordered. "I think heavy harness with a steady horse at his side will quiet him down." It did, and the colt trained so well that he went on to be a winner at the races.

One of the early photographs shows Harry Duffy, Second Whip, mounted on "Goldie Garmer". This blaze-faced bay of high metabolism and irascible temper, when so willed, could throw any rider. One day in front of the low-roofed bank stable at the club (since destroyed by fire), "Goldie" tossed Dick Merrick out of the saddle. A wag reporting the incident said, "Dick went up so high he landed on the stable roof". The same Dick Merrick (who was always the derring-do) is credited with the honor of being the only man who ever climbed, unassisted, to the top of the big mantle in the tap room. Another distinction goes to Joseph Devereux. Riding his pony in a drag one day, a formidable cattle bar blocked the hunt in the Jones Mill Road territory causing several refusals. Up rode Joe and clicking to Mingo, he sailed over the barrier. The M. F. H. witnessing the performance, then and there declared the boy an honorary member of the hunt. A serious accident was narrowly averted when the mount of Shirley Sudduth, one of the Whips, stumbled at a fence and turned a complete somersault, horse and rider landing with a jolt. Closely following was the groom of Colonel Dunn, Acting Master for the day. For a moment it looked as if the groom's mount would land on the prostrate forms of Shirley and his horse, but clever horsemanship succeeded in avoiding a serious mix-up.

The Hunt's Domain

The country hunted by the Chevy Chase Hounds was as fair and extensive as any one could wish. With the Club as the base of a vast arc, the domain, dotted by comfortable farmsteads, spread for miles to the east, north and west into gently rolling hills, almost endless fields of pasture and tillable lands, broken by large forests and winding streams. Galloping over the pastures was exceedingy fine, and the fences and stone walls were not beyond the capacity of a tolerably able horse. Very little wire, and that paneled at appropriate places. In height the obstacles averaged from three to four feet, the latter not being too difficult if there was a fair take-off and landing. With "good hands" and a firm seat on the rider's part, and a "will to go" on the horse's part, there was no pleasanter or safer country to hunt over, and in the autumn the russett oaks, golden hued maples, and the fiery red poison ivy vines made a fascinating scene.

The 1906 season started with a bang and The Post of November 5 gave a merry account of the occasion:

Chevy Chase Club Holds Its Initial Meet
Score of Riders Take Part

Chase of Elusive Anise Seed Bag by the Recently Imported English Foxhounds a Successful Affair—Well-Known Horsemen and Women Take the Jumps in Seven-Mile Dash

---

"And the horn of the hunter is heard on the hill."

A pack of 25 couples of English hounds, foam-flecked, and yelping at every bound, dashing up hill and down dale, through bramble and into thickets, closely followed by a merry party of enthusiastic pink-coated men and women in riding habits, all mounted on spirited hunting horses and taking scores of hazardous jumps and galloping at breakneck speed through the open country, with a windup and jollification at the clubhouse. Such was the opening meet of the hunting season at the Chevy Chase Club yesterday afternoon.

The initial event of the season, following the drag hounds, was a most successful affair, the hunt covering 7 miles of ever-changing country and roadway, and ending without serious mishap. About twenty men and women, all well up in horsemanship, and representing official, military and social circles, followed the hounds. The party was headed by Mr. Clarence Moore, the popular master of the hounds, and a daring horseman, who led the chase at a lively clip.

Some of Those in Scarlet

Among those who rode were the master, on Charles O'Malley; Mr. C. H. L. Johnston, on Red Gauntlet; Mr. J. A. C. Palmer, on Devil-to-get; Mr. A. B. Legare, on Gray Lady; Mr. Blanchard on The Marquis; Admiral and Miss Brownson, Mr. F. L. Huidekoper, on Ordessu; Mr. S. P. Knut, on the old veteran, Twilight, and Capt. Sowerby and Mr. Inness, from the British embassy. In attendance were the Huntsman, on Masterpiece; the first Whip, on Lord Craven; the second Whip, on Oakley, and the second horseman on Calenda. There were many automobiles and carriages grouped around the club as the hounds started away, and many followed them down the road and viewed the going away of the field. Among the spectators were Gen. Clarence Edwards and the Count de Chambrun, while Mr. and Mrs. William Henry followed the field as long as the roads ran in the vicinity of the drag.

The hounds were taken from the kennels to the Chevy Chase Club where the field had gathered, and at 3:30 went up the road to the field just across from the Chevy Chase Seminary, where the start of the drag had been laid. After being cast a couple of times by the

Meet of the Chevy Chase Hunt, near Tennallytown. Courtesy Mrs. Arthur A. Snyder.

Red Fox Vixen and Cubs.

Red Fox Vixen and Cubs. From an original drawing by Benson B. Moore.

The Old Clubhouse on a summer's day. Courtesy William C. DeLacy.

Tweet Tweet, current champion American foxhound. Courtesy Potomac Hunt. Photo by Freudy.

Huntsman, they struck the scent and went away, down the hill to the east of the railway, to the first fence of the season, which was taken bravely, while the hounds started through the woods and around the old Dunlop place, which they circled, coming out on the north side and crossing the railroad there. Here the hounds went at fault, but were laid on again in a few minutes, and ran to the road north of the lake, where a check was made, until the place of Mr. G. Thomas Dunlop was reached.

Hunters Scorn the Gaps

There the scent was again caught, and the field went away, scorning the gaps in the fences after getting their nerve well up on the five good stiff ones they had already taken. They jumped out onto the place of Mr. Dove; then ran through Woodmont, across the Rockville turnpike, over Mr. Nailor's farm, through the old Goldsborough place, then breathing a little more freely, for the Goldsborough place has the old-fashioned kind of fences on it, out onto Mr. Stock's farm, and through to West Chevy Chase, where the drag had been picked up.

Although more than 25 jumps were taken over rail fences and ditches, and the party penetrated a dence thicket, there was practically no "grief" in the run. It is understood that Mr. Knut was unseated, but landed on a soft spot and escaped injury. Mr. Moore injured one of his thumbs on a fence rail while protecting the rest of his body from injury when his hunter refused a jump. The jump was later taken by Mr. Moore's thoroughbred.

The hunt ended near Somerset, Maryland, and the party galloped across country to the club house, where their arrival was announced with vociferous blowing of horns.

The Master Well Satisfied

Mr. Moore said after the hunt he was well satisfied with the day's sport, and declared all the members of the party had had a great time. He said the ground was rather too hard and dry for English hounds to follow the scent well, but he was gratified over the performance of the hounds in their first tryout in this country.

From now on the hounds will be taken out four days a week, the drag pack on Wednesdays and Saturdays and the fox pack on Mondays and Thursdays, though the latter will not start until there has been some rain, as the ground is too dry now. The meets for the rest of the month have been arranged, and the hunt cards sent out, and from the brilliancy of the first meet, both as to field and spectators, they will prove most popular. Some of these meets held close in can be seen very nicely, the one at Brightwood on next Wednesday, in particular, is very accessible.

The fields should be big also, for the interest in riding and hunting especially has been revived to a large extent. It is not only the members of the Chevy Chase Club who have the privilege of hunting with the Chevy Chase hounds, but the hunt committee extends a general invitation to all who are fond of the sport to come and join the field, and the Chevy Chase Club extends the privilege and use of the club house on hunt days to subscribers to the pack who may not be members of the Club.

The following is the program for the remainder of November, as announced by Mr. Moore, the Master:

Monday,	8	Wheaton, Md., fox hounds
Wednesday,	10	Brightwood, drag hounds
Thursday,	11	Beane, Md., fox hounds
Saturday,	13	Tennallytown power house, drag hounds
Monday,	15	Garret Park, Md., fox hounds
Wednesday,	17	Bethesda, Md., drag hounds
Thursday,	18	Potomac, Md., fox hounds
Saturday,	20	Pierce's Mill, drag hounds
Monday,	22	Burnt Mills, Md., fox hounds
Wednesday,	24	Fort Myer, Va., drag hounds
Thursday,	25	Chevy Chase Club, fox hounds (Thanksgiving Day, 11 a.m.)
Saturday,	27	Chevy Chase Lake, drag hounds
Monday,	29	Cabin John, Md., fox hounds.

The drag hounds will meet at 3:30 p.m., and the fox hounds at 10 a.m. except on Thanksgiving Day, when they will meet at 11 a.m.

A Rich Program

In these days of quick transportation by horse vans and trailers, it is amazing the long distances the likes of Falstaff, Bachelor, Dancer, Spencer, Dragon, Gallant and the good bitches Rapture, Rapid, Gossip, Daphne, Velvet, Relish, and Bertha (all entered in Bob's fox hound studbook, with their whelping dates, sires and dams) were "roaded" to outlying meets, and one can visualize the Huntsman and Whips, often over frozen country roads, riding to fixtures at Rockville, Glen P. O., Chain Bridge, Great Falls and Potomac in Maryland, and to Falls Church and Langley in Virginia. From a hunting man's standpoint, it is only fair to say that the program which Mr. Moore so opulently provided could easily have absorbed the sporting capabilities of a club with a membership several times that of Chevy Chase. For those who wished to hunt the fox the menu was rich and varied, and the same can be said as regards the drags. At both the Metropolitan and Chevy Chase Clubs, the M. F. H. was constantly offering mounts to any friends who wished to participate, and however small the fields the meets always took place as scheduled.

A Meet in Rock Creek Park

'Way back yonder the Park was not the highly restricted area it has since become, hence there was no objection when the M. F. H. selected.

as he often did, Pierce Mill for a meeting place. A large gallery was out to see us off that day and Mr. Moore was busy acknowledging the greetings of friends and the kind words they were saying about the horses and hounds.

On this occasion I was riding a blood horse of my own named Navy Blue, and Mr. Moore had the leg up on Masterpiece. After the pleasant amenities, which are customary at every meet, Mr. Moore gave the signal and Bob Curran, with the two Whips, laid the hounds on the drag. They went away like a bat out of hell and the field followed. After several miles of hard galloping the hounds fled into the upper park where the scent followed the edge of Rock Creek and where the excited cries of hounds, reverberating in the hills and rocky cliffs, seemed a never-ending record of sporting music.

One Cold Ducking

Racing for all we were worth, for a good horse really loves to follow hounds, we came to a meadow where young trees had sprung up. Navy Blue and the other horses glided among them with the skill of polo ponies when, apparently set to bear to the left of a tree, Navy Blue suddenly swerved to the right, catching me off balance and dumping me into the inhospitable creek. My cap flew off and I floundered about completely soaked. Several riders stood by to help me, but finding I was uninjured (except in my pride), they galloped off with typical banter of the hunting field. Groping my way to the bank I squeezed as much water and sand as I could from my clothing, and chilled to the spine, hurried to the road where a passing motorist kindly carried me home. In the meantime hounds, horses and riders ran the course and finished at Kensington, including the frolicsome Navy Blue.

A Brave Diana

It is worthy of note that in 1909 Miss Brownson was the only feminine member of the Hunt who had the courage to ride cross-saddle. A photo shows her so mounted, erect as an Indian, on her alert, bob-tailed hunter, in front of the Club ready for the chase. We also hear of Miss Katherine Elkins and Miss Mathilde Townsend, as well as Miss Harriet Wadsworth, being in the field, each having her own stable and string of hunters. Probably the most famous rider among the women was Mrs. Herbert Wadsworth, of the Genesee Valley Hunt, whose exploits in long distance riding were such as to put to blush some of the men. Miss Gaff and Miss Jackson, however, were on the missing list that season, as both had committed matrimony and were absent from Washington. One of the most popular riders was Capt. C. F. G. Sowerby, Naval Attache of the British Embassy, who had hunted a good deal in England and seemed to find the Chevy Chase Hounds very much to his taste. Major W. A. Wadsworth, Henry T. Oxnard, James F. Barbour, Capt. Larz Anderson, Senator Newlands, Walter Tuckerman, George Dunlop, Montgomery Blair and William C. Eustis, all seemed to relish the winey air atop a good horse when the pack was rattling along at a lively pace. Mr. Blair was a great hand for breaking colts.

Members Proud of Curran

"Happy the man who, with unrival'd speed, can pass his fellows, and with pleasure view the struggling pack."

Somerville, The Chase (1727)

The hunt members were proud of Bob Curran and fond of pointing out his resemblance to the picture of Tom Firr, Huntsman of the Quorn

Hunt for more than 30 years, and reputed the greatest exponent of his art that England ever knew. Shirley Sudduth and Pete Curran, the whips, were also held in high esteem. Since the regular hunting season does not begin until November, Bob, to insure hounds being fit, would start them in August on "cub" hunting, in which young foxes, called cubs, as well as young hounds, were given a taste of the sport. On these excursions, which took place around sun-up, Bob, who was as meticulous for the niceties of attire as the M.F.H. himself, always appeared, along with Shirley and Pete, in cub hunting livery — light khaki coat, with scarlet collar and breeches. Mr. Moore, a keen follower of the English style of hunting, required Bob to carry on exactly as if he were in the old country, using the calls that have been heard for generations. "Cubbing" this morning are three and one half couple of old hounds and five couple of young hounds—seventeen in all — the custom being always to hunt an odd number.

Now an old hound speaks, a sharp tentative note, and Bob, satisfied it is a fox scent, shouts "Huic, huic, huic, to Rachel, Huic" (pronounced "hike, hike, hike"), and when the whole pack has gone to Rachel and pushed the quarry into the open, where they can really rate him, Bob cries "Huic! huic! huic! forrard, forrard, forrard," using his voice cheeringly, for fox hounds are sensitive creatures and love to be cajoled. Our foray being a cub hunt, the pack is allowed only a short run or two because the puppies are not yet hardened to serious work.

A Fine Art

Bob Curran (who passed away in 1935) elevated fox hunting to the status of a fine art. With experienced (entered) hounds out for a chase Bob, in order to find his fox, always kept in mind such things as temperature, wind, sun and ground conditions, and Bob claimed his instinct told him where a fox was apt to lie.

If the country happened to be covered with snow, Bob knew a fox would like to doze beneath a pine tree on bare warm ground; on a day with the air getting colder and the wind rising, Reynard favored a protective shock of corn to curl up in; but come a mild, sunny day, with the temperature rising, he might be found in a shady spot under a vine-covered fence line.

Bob kept his eye on any crows, sheep or cattle he encountered, for their behavior frequently furnished clues to the quarry's line of flight. His hounds, by the way they worked, suggested the quality of the scent, which might be breasthigh, holding, or poor, and whether they were chasing a red or gray fox. If the quarry went to earth, Bob had to decide whether to grant sanctuary or dig him out. After all, it is a blood sport, and some huntsmen to keep hounds ruthlessly keen deem it necessary that they taste blood occasionally. The most humiliating thing that can happen to a Huntsman, however, is to be unable to account for his fox; meaning that he has neither gone to earth or been killed, but has simply eluded his enemies by disappearing without a trace.

Equally disappointing is a "blank" day when the Huntsman, with a thinning number of followers, spends hour after hour in field or forest "drawing" for scent. But never a whimper comes from his pack. At such a time everybody is willing to settle for the faintest of cold trails in the hope that hounds can develop it into a worthwhile run. If, finally, with the sun sinking, nothing happens, then wearily back to kennels. All of which sometimes happens to the best of huntsmen and finest of packs, and leaves fox hunting, as it has always been, a tangy, uncertain venture in pursuit of one of the craftiest little gamins that ever caught a field rat or robbed a hen roost.

Heythrop Plunder, current champion English foxhound. Courtesy The Chronicle, Middleburg, Va. Photo by Frank H. Meads.

Miss Frances Moore, keen and ready. From the Chapin collection.

The Huntsman Reminisces

"Old John Peel", said Bob Curran one summer day at the Kennels while the hounds stretched out in the shade, "was the most famous fox hunter that ever lived, and I often find myself humming 'D'ye ken John Peel with his coat so gray, d'ye ken John Peel at the break of day, d'ye ken John Peel when he's far, far away with his hounds and his horn in the morn-ing?' And you know, they say of him that he would drink, would Peel, 'till he couldn't stand, and then they would clap him on his horse and away he would go as right as a fiddle."

Bob, a small, powerful man, was in a jovial mood and his gray eyes twinkled as he continued: "Being a huntsman, foxes have always interested me; of all animals he is the most mysterious. You've heard the old rhyme: "A lean horse for a long race, a spotted pig for a boar, a red fox for a hard chase and white oak planks for a door." Yes, the red fox is the long running, tough and courageous one, in contrast to the timid, faint-hearted gray. A game old red knows his country intimately and is not afraid to strike out boldly, sometimes going off as far as 10 or 15 miles. He knows where the dens, trails and crossings are, and with his ample tricks and ravelings takes every advantage in frustrating his enemies. He is a faithful husband and father, and should hounds press him hard when his vixen and their cubs are in the home den, he will perish rather than reveal their whereabouts."

The Vier's Mill Fox

The Huntsman was now warmed up to his favorite sport, and it was clear he had a story to tell. "One cold, cloudy February day awhile back, we had a hunt I will never forget," he said. "Only a few were out because rain had fallen during the night and the going was sloppy—Mr. Moore on Masterpiece, Miss Frances Moore on her black mare, Mr. Alex Legare on Gray Lady, Mr. Dion Kerr with his new chestnut horse and one or two others. I was on Thunder; the Whips, Shirley Sudduth with the leg up on Mr. Jorrocks, and Pete Curran on Lord Craven.

"The meet had been fixed for ten o'clock at the Garrett Park railroad station, and promptly at the hour we moved across the tracks and cast hounds in heavy woods where I felt a fox might be lying up in a hollow log after a night on his feeding trails. The hounds went to work at once. 'Try up old fellows,' I called, 'Push 'im up in there, try!' and when a first season bitch opened on a rabbit, I cracked my whip and shouted, 'War' hare, Sweet lips! What are you at! Get back, War' hare then!' It began to look like we were drawing blank; then I see one of the whips, who had been stationed at the edge of the woods to watch for a fox that might try to steal away, waving his cap and I knew he had viewed. I called the pack and put them on, the entire ten and a half couple in full chorus and I blowing the gone away, gone, gone, ah-ah a-w-a-y. This fellow carried us for three miles, then doubled back and raced toward Rockville. Mr. Moore shouted 'It's that old Vier's Mill red, and we are in for a burner. Spare your horses all you can, but don't get too far behind or hounds will lose you.' The hounds knew they had a 'tartar' too, and as he twisted and turned to throw them off, their notes took on a savage tone. A half mile from Rockville he veered to the right and sensing his danger crossed Rock Creek below the Halpine Road and headed for Aspen Hill, checking the pack by running through cattle and sheep, dense banks of honeysuckle, piney woods, and the very edge of the old mica mine. The checks were welcome, nevertheless, for they gave the horses a breather and afforded the riders a chance to study hound work at close range.

Big Country

"With everybody riding well up, including two farmers who had joined us, he passed Aspen Hill on his right, breezed across the Olney Pike, and pointed straight for the big country to the East, eventually bringing us to some of the finest grass lands in the State. In this perfect setting for a genuine fox race he forced hounds to really extend themselves. Over and around the huge Heurich, Rapley and Wimsatt farms he coursed, not a let up in field after field, but an out and out galloping picnic, yet never affording us a fleeting view.

"Our phantom-like racer had now come to the limits of his regular beat where the terrain was familiar to him in the smallest detail. But he was no fool; he knew the dangers of invading the strange country beyond where the pack would have him at their mercy. Moreover, his concealed den on the bluff overlooking the mill race began to beckon. The red one responded. Turning back, he started for home, not crying Uncle, mind you, for he still had plenty of speed and strategy left.

"As he sailed along, keen and jaunty, his foxy brain searching for a spot to confuse and delay us, he thought of a nearby farm house and when we reached the place we found he had pulled a fast one, an excited woman informing us that the moment she heard the hunt approaching she ran to the back porch just in time to see the fox dash through the barnyard scattering ducks and chickens in every direction, her little terrier nipping his heels until he leaped a picket fence and disappeared. Of course, the trick worked out as he had planned, the rank odors of the yard completely foiling his scent and holding us up until Falstaff and Bertha recovered the line. As the clamorous hounds went away Mr. Moore shouted 'They're warning him to step faster or hole up, Bob.'

"We were shortly to enjoy one of the unforgettable highlights of riding to hounds, a thrill ever old and ever new. Pushing our horses to the limit we came to a big meadow where Paint Branch meandered through a stand of swamp willows. Here we viewed the fox on the edge of the timber being mobbed by a noisy flock of crows. Y'know, there is a strange quality about a running fox, something mysterious and beautiful. Silent and stealthy, he paid no attention to his feathery tormentors, but skimmed over the soggy ground as graceful as a swallow, his only worries the bugling hounds and cries of Tally-Ho, Tally-Ho!

"After tallying the fugitive a series of mishaps struck us. Mr. Legare's mare lost all four shoes in a quicksand, Mr. Kerr broke a stirrup strap, which Shirley promptly made good by a spare he carried, and Miss Francis' mare, stepping in a muskrat hole, let her down, but with the help of Mr. Kerr she quickly remounted.

A Blazing Finish

"His scent hung sweetly on the frosty air and hounds ran as if glued to his line. Into heavy thickets, under hickories and oaks edging little pools of water, scurried the crafty beggar. Breaking cover he crossed a pasture and came to a stone wall. When we got to it, hounds threw up their heads and ceased tonguing, puzzled by the complete loss of scent. Up to this point the chase had been an even thing, and I realized that he would beat us if we did not make a quick recovery. I lifted hounds and galloped

46

them down-wind to a small creek where the wall ended, hounds still mute and as perplexed as I was.

"My judgment indicated that the fox had run the wall, but how and where he jumped off was the big question. Probably made a mighty leap, I argued, and landed across the creek. It was a shallow bit of water, and as I was spurring Thunder through it, Sailor, a hound with plenty of "fox sense", beat me across. After ranging in the brush for a few minutes, Sailor picked up the line and let out a roar; the whole pack rushed to him and were off, scent breast high and hounds running like smoke.

"As we had chased the red rascal some twenty miles, our horses were beginning to lean on their bits—a sure sign of fatigue—and they were covered with mud and foam and we had to steady them at walls and fences. It was now or never, and as hounds burst into an old stubble field, I rose in my stirrups and called, 'Break him up, yoi-yoicks, drive on my beauties.' At that Sailor, Ruler, and Spottswood surged from the screaming pack and forged ahead in a booming challenge; it was like the last quarter in a horse race when breeding and condition begin to tell. They push hard and soon have him in sight, his head down, tongue far out and brush dragging. In no time at all they are at his flanks; he turns and snaps at them, and they pull him down on the Old Ford and Graham farm on the Vier's Mill Road, north of Wheaton, about a mile from his den. I sound the kill notes, leap from my steaming horse, beat off the pack and cut the mask and brush from the carcass. Mr. Moore was right at my side and I said, 'Sir, that was a tough, hard running fox, but he wasn't good enough today', and he replied, 'Quite true, Bob. I never saw hounds work better. That last hour was blazing, and they deserved to have him.' Then Mr. Moore orders me to hand the brush to Miss Frances and keep the mask myself."

Blowing Hounds Home

Taking a pull on his pipe, Bob resumed his story: "After the Master had passed the flask around, he took a good swig himself and said to me, 'That's enough for today, Bob, blow hounds home.' I sound the long, mournful notes and we shove off at a sharp trot. When we arrive at the kennels there is Mr. Moore's big limousine waiting, and he and Miss Frances and several others get in and are driven to the Club. I look the hounds over as they are eating the hot feed which the kennel men have prepared, and give orders for attending to any that are injured. On my way to the house, a stud groom excitedly reports Roxanne has foaled a beautiful colt, and I go to the stables where I find the mare on her feet and the youngster coming along in good shape. As we had left the kennels at eight o'clock and returned at three, we were seven hours in the saddle, jumped everything we came to, and best of all, accounted for our fox."

"Is that the fox head that hangs in your house?" someone asked. "It is," replied Bob, "I hope my children always take good care of it."

[NOTE — the writer is glad to report that during a recent visit to Marrian Curran's farm, on the Kemp Mill Road, he had the pleasure of seeing the trophy—a snarling fox baring his sharp teeth in defiant challenge.]

The M. F. H. Goes Abroad

Come the fall of 1911 and we find the M. F. H. shoving off for another of his numerous trips abroad. However, before sailing, according to Marrian Curran who had the story from his father, Mr. Moore purchased Belmont, a historic estate near Leesburg, Virginia, and had instructed Bob to have everything ready to move there in the following spring when he expected to return home. What Mr. Moore's plans were for Belmont, with its rambling stone mansion, ample stables, paddocks and acreage, we can only conjecture, but it is worthy to note that he did not resign as M. F. H. While abroad he purchased twelve Welsh pony mares and a stallion, eight Irish hunters and ten diminutive Kerry cattle, although Rock Creek Farms already was loaded with a score or more horses, countless hounds, Dalmatians, French poodles, Dachshunds, toy bull dogs, English sheep dogs and English bull dogs.

Death of Masterpiece.

For $150 Mr. Moore had picked up from a Virginia farmer a rangy bay horse which he named Masterpiece. Bob Curran schooled the bargain horse until he was the best mannered and most honest performing hunter either he or Mr. Moore had ever ridden. Masterpiece could and did take a seven foot, two inch fence without a tick. At about the time Mr. Moore was leaving for England, a field trial was being held at Dawsonville, Maryland, and the Chevy Chase Hunt's English bred hounds were beaten by the home bred pack of a local farmer. It was on this occasion that Masterpiece was fatally injured. Bob Curran decided to show the Marylanders what a real horse could do; he put the gallant hunter at a five foot gate which began to swing just as Masterpiece extended himself in mid-air, causing the horse to come crashing down on the top rail groaning in pain. With tears streaming down his face, Bob held the horse's head cradled in his arms until late in the night when Masterpiece expired. It was a bad omen.

The Titanic Sinks

After spending the winter abroad, during which he acquired a new supply of English hounds and attended the Liverpool Grand National at Aintree, Mr. Moore sailed for New York on the Titanic in April, 1912, and perished in that crushing tragedy of the sea along with 1502 other passengers. "When the ship struck the iceberg Mr. Moore and a group of men were in the First Class smoking room on A Deck, and as usual, it was a very mixed group. Around one table sat Archie Butt, President Taft's military aide; Clarence Moore, the traveling Master of Hounds; Harry Widener, son of the Philadelphia streetcar magnate, and William Carter, another Main Liner. They were winding up a small dinner given by Widener's father in honor of Captain Edward J. Smith, the ship's commander. The Captain had left early, the ladies had been packed off to bed, and now the men were enjoying a final cigar before turning in too. The conversation wandered from politics to Clarence Moore's adventures in West Virginia, the time he helped interview the old feuding mountaineer Anse Hatfield." [From A Night to Remember, by Walter Lord. A legend has grown up that Mr. Moore was bringing the newly acquired hounds with him on the Titanic. However, since there was no room on board for the hounds, the man in charge was luckily forced to bring them over on a later ship.]

One of the Smartest Hunts

The Hunt under Mr. Moore's guidance was famous for being one of the smartest in America, and the scarlet coats and black velvet collars were popular all through the surrounding country where the farmers, many of whom kept a few hounds of their own and prospered through the sale of provender to the Hunt, were always ready to extend welcome greetings. For the country folk Mr. Moore had the utmost consideration; all damage to their crops and fencing caused by the Hunt was immediately paid for, and to improve the quality of their horses the services of his noble black stallion, Columbia, were available without cost. All of which merely points up the fact that everyone knows (or should know), that hunting could not exist in any country without the cooperation and good will of the farmers.

And it was Mr. Moore who had an artist paint the shields of noted American companion hunts that hang in the tap room of the Club where, surrounded by golf and tennis trophies, they contribute a bit of nostalgic color reminiscent of the old days during which the Chevy Chase Hunt, with lasting credit to itself and in spite of its inevitable ups and downs, played an important part in the history of fox hunting in the country around Washington.

A Lordly Master

Of Clarence Moore, we can justly say he will always be remembered as a lordly master and one of the great sportsmen of his time.

After his death, Charles H. L. Johnston was elected Acting Master and hunted the hounds until 1916, when the Hunt passed into history. Next came the Riding and Hunt Club, which in many ways was a lively counterpart of the old Washington Hunt of the 1830's, and like the latter, always sparked for "divilment and divarsion". But that is another story. When the Riding and Hunt outfit evolved into the Potomac Hunt under the joint mastership of our General Harry H. Semmes and Dr. Fred R. Sanderson, for many an old timer it was a great consolation to know hounds would still be crying the fox in the rolling hills of Maryland where Bob Curran's melliferous voice and the tuneful notes of Sarah and Sporting, Comrade and Sailor of the Chevy Chase were often heard in the long, long ago.

CPSIA information can be obtained
at www.ICGtesting.com
Printed in the USA
BVOW06*0158221216
471483BV00008B/74/P